The Feeling Child

What impact does children's emotional development and well-being have on their capacity to learn? How do you provide learning experiences that meet the developmental needs of every child in your care?

The Feeling Child thoughtfully discusses the key principles of children's emotional and behavioural development alongside descriptions of everyday practice. It clearly explains how a child's early experiences influence their particular behaviours towards different people and different situations.

Throughout the book, Maria Robinson considers the key characteristics of effective learning and shows how play is one of the key mechanisms that children use in their discovery of themselves and the world around them. These characteristics are then applied to integral aspects of early years practice to help practitioners to:

- support children to come to new understandings in safe yet challenging ways;
- understand the ways in which children may approach or withdraw from learning opportunities;
- reflect on their own teaching methods to encourage children's engagement, motivation and creativity through effective observation and planning;
- engage with parents and carers to help support children's learning at home whilst maintaining the values of the family;
- celebrate the uniqueness of each child and provide learning experiences that are appropriate for individuals with particular learning needs, be they physical, emotional or cognitive, to ensure that every child has an equal opportunity to succeed.

Emphasising the importance of understanding the theory that underpins children's emotional development, this accessible text shows practitioners how they can use this knowledge to provide learning opportunities that nourish children's thinking and creative skills.

Maria Robinson is a lecturer, counsellor, trainer and adviser in early years development, with a total of 20 years' experience including working originally as a health visitor and subsequently as a tutor in further and higher education. She currently works independently, offering training and workshops to a wide range of professionals such as early years practitioners, social workers, trainee and qualified teachers in both mainstream and additional support needs education. Her particular areas of interest are the emotional development of children, attachment, brain development and links between all aspects of development and the use of observations.

Foundations of Child Development
Series Editor: Pamela May

An understanding of child development is at the heart of good early years practice. The four books in this exciting new series each take a detailed look at a major strand of child development – cognitive, social, physical and emotional – and aim to provide practitioners with the knowledge and understanding they need to plan ways of working with children that are developmentally appropriate. Clearly linking theory to everyday practice they explain why practitioners teach in certain ways and show how they can provide learning experiences that will help children to become competent and enthusiastic learners. Whilst the series allows for an in-depth study of each of the four major areas of development individually, it also demonstrates that they are, in reality, intertwined and indivisible.

Titles in this series:

The Feeling Child

Laying the foundations of confidence and resilience

Maria Robinson

Routledge
Taylor & Francis Group

LONDON AND NEW YORK

First published 2014
by Routledge
2 Park Square, Milton Park, Abingdon, Oxon OX14 4RN

and by Routledge
711 Third Avenue, New York, NY 10017

Routledge is an imprint of the Taylor & Francis Group, an informa business

British Library Cataloguing in Publication Data
A catalogue record for this book is available from the British Library

Library of Congress Cataloging in Publication Data
A catalog record for this book has been requested

ISBN: 978-0-415-52121-5 (hbk)
ISBN: 978-0-415-52122-2 (pbk)
ISBN: 978-0-203-12205-1 (ebk)

Typeset in Bembo and Frutiger
by Wearset Ltd, Boldon, Tyne and Wear

MIX
Paper from responsible sources
FSC
www.fsc.org   FSC® C013056

Printed and bound in Great Britain by
TJ International Ltd, Padstow, Cornwall

Contents

Acknowledgements

This book is dedicated to the memory of my beloved husband, Stuart, who died from mesothelioma in April 2012. A wonderful, courageous man, who helped me through all my work and studies, was my best friend, healer of my hurts and deepest love.

I wish to acknowledge the wonderful support, and patience, of Pam May and the great editorial skills of John May. Also the publishers for their patience in waiting for this book. I also wish to acknowledge and give grateful thanks to all the families I have worked with as a health visitor; they will never know how much they taught me. Also to all the students I encountered who were studying early years work and the amazing, dedicated colleagues I have met over the years. Thank you for all your support, encouragement and also absolute commitment to the well-being of young children.

Introduction to the series

Let us begin by considering two situations with which we are all probably familiar. Picture, if you will, a sandy beach. The sun is shining, there are gentle waves, little rock pools and a big cave. You have with you children aged six and three, a picnic, towels and buckets and spades. Having chosen your spot, you settle down with a rug and a good book, occasionally advising about the construction of the moat for the sand castle or checking out the dragons in the cave. The children come back occasionally to eat or for a drink, and there are the necessary breaks for loos and ice creams. By 4 p.m. everyone has had a perfect day; you included. No one has cried, there were no squabbles and the children are happily tired enough to ensure a good night's sleep. For days and weeks to come they remember the 'best holiday ever' as they reminisce about the castles they constructed and the dragons they frightened.

Now, transfer these same two children to a local supermarket. Imagine the scene here. In my experience the situation starts badly as I issue the firm instruction 'not to touch anything' as we enter the store, and rapidly goes downhill as one child finds the strawberry yoghurts but the other wants the blueberry ones. I want the mixed pack because they are on offer; a three-way dispute is quickly under way. The smaller child is transferred to the child seat in the trolley, kicking and wailing loudly, and many mothers look at me with either sympathy or distaste as this noisy gang proceeds with the shopping. Matters are not helped by the sweets displayed at the checkout at child level, which this cross granny does not consider either of them has deserved.

Why are these two scenarios so very different? The answer lies in the ways that children are hard-wired to learn about their world and to make sense of it. This process is called child development. Children are born with a set of strategies and they apply these strategies wherever they find themselves. One of the ways children learn is by using their senses; they need to touch things that interest them to find out about them. That is fine when they are digging in the sand on the beach

Figure I.1 *Checking out the dragons in the cave*

and collecting shells, but not nearly so acceptable when investigating packets of crisps in a supermarket. Children are also hard-wired to learn actively, that is, by exploring what is around them. Again, great when looking for dragons in caves, but not such a helpful strategy around the aisles in a shop.

So these books consider the strategies and other characteristics that all young children have, and consider how they can be developed and strengthened in the course of young children's everyday learning.

This series of books is about the process of learning and not the content of learning. Each book describes a separate area of a young child's development and how their relationships and experiences affect the process of that development. Each of the four books takes one aspect and considers it in depth.

- ***The Feeling Child:*** *Laying the foundations of confidence and resilience.* In this book I consider children's emotional and behavioural development.
- ***The Thinking Child:*** *Laying the foundations of understanding and competence.* In this book Pam May considers children's cognitive and intellectual development.

- **The Growing Child:** *Laying the foundations of active learning and physical health.* In this book Clair Stevens considers children's physical and motor development.
- **The Social Child:** *Laying the foundations of relationships and language.* In this book Toni Buchan considers children's social and language development.

Although each book takes one strand of children's development and looks at it separately, this is purely for the purpose of study. In real life, of course, children use all aspects of their development together as they learn to sustain friendships and communicate, grow taller and stronger, deepen their understanding of concepts and morals and grow in self-confidence.

There are thought to be certain characteristics inherent in all children that enable development to proceed effectively. Two of these inborn characteristics, for example, are motivation and autonomy. They need to be matched by an environment which supports their expression and development. Children who thrive and learn well will find their innate characteristics supported by loving and knowledgeable adults in a challenging yet secure environment. This environment will respect the fact that children learn through first-hand experiences, through their senses and that they will usually be doing this actively. This is why the beach provides such an effective learning environment and the supermarket less so. On the beach children can use their strategies of active engagement. They are motivated by the exciting surroundings and can play with considerable freedom and autonomy. Here, one can see that their curiosity and capability of finding out about the world are perfectly matched by their environment.

This series will examine these ideas in depth. Established and current research threads through and underpins all the practical suggestion offered here. A theory is no use in isolation; it must always link to what happens to children wherever they are, every day. This is why these books will give the practitioner a chance to consider what implications their reading may have on their practice, as well as giving them sound, evidence-based understanding as to why certain ways of teaching and learning can be so successful.

Central to this series are some key beliefs about young children. These include the premise that:

- children are potentially strong and autonomous learners
- they need loving and sensitive adults to be their companions
- children's view of themselves is key to their success as learners
- play is a powerful mechanism that enables children to develop their understandings
- what children can do should be the starting point of their future learning.

Perhaps these ideas are summed up most clearly in the last of the NYEYC principles:

> Children's experiences shape their motivation and approaches to learning, such as persistence, initiative and flexibility; in turn these dispositions and behaviours affect their learning and development.[1]

These principles are about not *what* children learn but *how* they learn and consequently, how they are best taught. They are reflected in the Early Years Foundation Stage (EYFS) document which is currently under review.[2]

Happily, the review places much emphasis on the characteristics of effective learning that we considered above, and it is these that we will be examining closely. Each book will discuss those characteristics which apply most closely to the strand of development being considered in the book but, of course, many of these will appear throughout the series. Each book will have chapters reflecting the EYFS emphasis on aspects of effective learning, in particular:

- play and exploration
- active learning
- creativity and critical thinking.

Other chapters will cover aspects of practice common to all settings, such as observing children's learning, engaging with families and how to provide for the different learning styles of girls and boys. Finally, there will be a chapter that critically examines the notion of 'school readiness'. Each author will explore what it means to be 'school ready' and how we may best support Foundation Stage children to take advantage of all that is on offer for them at key stage one.

Introduction to *The Feeling Child*

This book establishes a fundamental framework for all aspects of a child's ability to learn. It is fundamental because, as we may know or guess at, all our decision making, our attitudes to ourselves and others, motivation, belief, levels of commitment and persistence are all colour-washed by how we *feel*. Ask yourself, what might motivate you to try your hardest at your work or study? If you think carefully about it, you may find several aspects involved; this may include your attitude towards the work itself, or it may be that you want to progress further, or perhaps, deep down, you may fear failure or wish to please others and feel their approval. With all of us, our feelings and how they affect our behaviour influence every facet of our lives, including our motivation, our ability to empathise, our capacity to reflect, to engage with others or with an activity. Our feelings, therefore, profoundly influence our attitude and disposition for learning.

To summarise, what this book will discuss is how feelings in our earliest years shape our feelings of self-worth and self-esteem, and how the echoes of such experiences can reverberate throughout life. This is because we never lose the flavour of those experiences, although we may modify and adapt them in the light of new experiences as we grow.

Another aspect of the feeling child is that in order for a child to find out about themselves and the world around them, they need to explore. In other words, a child, literally and metaphorically feels their way into the world from the moment of birth and indeed before. Exploration and play therefore constitutes a crucial part of how a child begins to learn as the child literally reaches out to embrace their surroundings and thereby through all their senses discover what it is to be an individual human being, alive and living in their own particular environment.

Of course, a child is not in isolation; the role of adults, parents and other carers is paramount, in particular the role of early years practitioners and the necessity of the concepts of love and nurture to be inherent in the professional role.

We are feeling beings; feelings are powerful and an essential part of our humanity. What we feel about our experiences from the earliest moment of our lives can set the background theme to the time we have on the stage of life.

CHAPTER 1

Setting the scene

Recently, while listening to the radio, my attention was caught by an item about stress. Stress had apparently become the number one reason for absence from work and the topic was generating a great deal of discussion. However, continuing to listen, I realised that although people were apparently talking about 'stress', what they appeared to be actually describing were their feelings in response to various adverse life circumstances. It seemed as if their experiences of anger, sadness or fear were being lumped together under this 'stress umbrella' rather than the identification of the specific responses to their experiences. This is not to undermine in any way the reality of stress itself which, in its purest form, is anything which causes a disturbance in how we feel, think and behave.

Thinking about this further, I realised that there is another way in which we appear to lump together a range of possible feelings – the common usage of the term 'depression'. People can be heard to say that they are 'a bit depressed', when in fact what they might be feeling is worried and/or sad, fearful or anxious. Again, this does not in any way undermine the reality of depressive illness, which is all-consuming and frightening in the levels of hopelessness and despair that such a condition can produce. Nevertheless, it is interesting to reflect on why we appear to want to give a medical flavour to our feelings. It is as if calling our sadness, depression or our feelings of helplessness and powerlessness 'stress' somehow validates them, perhaps making them more acceptable to others and thereby we may feel more able to seek help and/or behave in particular ways.

This led me on to wonder if we have forgotten that as human beings we come into the world already equipped with a range of emotions (albeit initially in very simple forms) which tend to be universally acknowledged and recognised,[1] and which, as noted in the introduction, colour-wash all our thoughts and behaviour. These common emotions are happiness, sadness, fear, anger, disgust and surprise, and we express them in our faces (including the most subtle movements of eyebrows, mouth curve and nostril widening or narrowing), our eyes and also through body language. However, the latter can be more problematical as the same movement can mean different things in different cultures! Nevertheless there appear to be some aspects of body language which retain a similar meaning, such as cowering in submission; a signal shared across the animal as well as human kingdom. The common language of emotions, therefore, especially facial expression and eye gaze, provides a bridge of communication between all humans, allowing us to feel a sense of connection with one another. This means that while no-one can feel exactly what you are feeling in any given situation, the shared understanding and what our outward behaviour may signify as to our inner state means that we can *empathise* with one another. Empathy and/or sympathetic understanding is crucial for cooperative behaviour and wards against cruelty and neglect, which leads us into the 'why' of feelings.

Why feel?

Why do we have the emotions described above and all those others which are often the result of a more complex interweaving of those basic strands? For example, jealousy is essentially a mix of fear of abandonment, sadness at potential loss and perhaps, more obvious, anger dependent on the particular context in which the feeling may be aroused. For example, seeing your loved one look favourably on someone else! Envy and resentment too often have their roots in fundamental ideas of not being 'good enough', which in turn masks sadness and/or anger at not feeling noticed and appreciated. It is a cliché, of course, but emotions are what makes us human and, as important, make us able to function. It may seem counter-intuitive, but they actually help us to think logically; without emotions we seem to have problems in making decisions and planning. Studies of people who have had parts of the brain damaged which are involved in the processing of emotions have been found to be severely curtailed in their ability to simply live from day to day. Logic is not all! This is because we feel *something* in response to everything we encounter and at its most basic level, circumstances/events can feel pleasant or unpleasant. Being human also means that we tend to want to repeat the pleasant experiences and avoid the unpleasant ones. This is an evolutionary safeguard on many levels (something tastes nice, eat it again; it tastes horrible, avoid it!); but this sensible action can also turn against us if what we find pleasurable actually harms us, such as too much alcohol, misuse of other drugs or risky behaviour. Of course, as we will discover, such behaviours are often a means of finding something, *anything* to help us feel better when daily life seems unbearable in some way. The brain, which is the arbiter of all our experiences, does not discriminate between what is good for us and what is not; it simply, as we shall see later in this chapter, processes information and provides the bedrock for our responses and behaviour.

There is another important aspect to the idea that we are born with feelings, and that is that our feelings are not created in a vacuum but are awakened by the circumstances in which we find ourselves; this awakening begins even before we are born as we develop in our mother's womb.[2] This suggests, in a very real sense, that each of us essentially creates our own particular reality dependent on the type of experiences we have and *how we respond to them*. Behaviour is therefore a result of our unique perception of ourselves and others and this perception is based on what we feel in response to our circumstances; with a dash of genetics thrown in.

Sing a song of childhood

> My soul is like a hidden orchestra; I do not know which instruments grind and play away inside of me, strings and harps, timbales and drums, I can only recognize myself as a symphony.[3]
>
> (Pessoa)

This wonderful quote is used by Damasio[4] and it encapsulates beautifully that the person we are, as child or adult, is a result of all the developmental factors combined within us: physical, cognitive, social and emotional. Just as a piece of music, sung or played, is the result of the combination of only eight notes, so our development is a combination of all these factors. This is why, although in this series these developmental factors are presented as separate issues, all the authors lay great stress on their ultimate integration. The importance of seeing development in a holistic way is vital as all too often the integrated nature of development has been overtaken by the particular perspective on development which may be fashionable at any one time. For example, the 'behaviourist' school which seemed to reduce human behaviour to a system of stimulus and response. While this perspective does have validity in that we do respond to stimuli in particular ways that can be repeated in a variety of contexts with similar aspects, it does not explain the how and why of such reactions and the reason why they can become repetitive. The growing realisation that this approach was not sufficient to understand human behaviour was followed by an emphasis on cognitive development, with emotions taking a distant back seat. In fact, the idea that emotions were important and not simply an inconvenient side issue has come to the fore only in the past two decades, when brain research has begun to reveal the power of those emotional circuits in our brains. An emphasis on a particular ideology or devotion to one particular theoretical perspective has meant that the issues surrounding a child's capacity to learn and adapt their behaviour in different situations can be viewed simply as a particular 'problem' rather than a reflection of what forces may be at work that influence the child's ultimate reaction to their circumstances.

Nevertheless, it is heartening that in the neuroscientific world at least (if not yet in the wider media), the reality of the influence of emotions/feelings on the overall developmental well-being of the child is increasingly recognised.[5] This shift is described as being based on research on three main categories: first, how our brains develop and, most importantly, what aspect of development appears to be most crucial in the early years; second, how we make and maintain relationships, in particular the role of attachment (crucial for human functioning); and third, how we learn to regulate or 'control' our own behaviour. Research in all these areas has highlighted the importance of the early years and crucially the response to the emotional behaviour shown by infants and very young children by their caretakers. Schore quotes extensively from huge amounts of research in all these areas and how they combine together to produce a child's feelings of self-worth and self-perception, and thereby lead on to how well the child can respond to their experiences; which, of course, includes their aptitude to learn.[6]

The issues that Schore mentions: neuroscience, attachment and self regulation, are like the three parts to a melody; individual and indivisible.

Understanding the brain

While Schore emphasizes the role of the brain, we must not forget that the brain is the 'processor' or arbiter of all the information we get from our bodily feelings which arise from our experiences. This includes bodily sensations, vision, hearing, touch and movement. Movement is our first 'communication', as in the womb we stretch, kick, suck, swallow, blink and feel all around our growing body, the sensation of the warm, watery world in which we develop. We also hear sound through our mother's tummy and especially the tone and pitch of her voice.

We hear other voices too, but hers is the one we are aware of the most,[7] so this section of the chapter will take a brief look at the role of the senses, as well as an outline of the workings of the brain.

There are some key points about our amazing and magical brains described by Robinson[8]; these are:

- The brain is possibly the most complex structure in the universe and our understanding of it is still in its infancy, in spite of the enormous strides in recent times in untangling some of its processes.

- The mind is embedded in the workings of the brain, but exactly how the processes of an organic structure evolve into the miracle of our understanding of a personal 'self' remains an ongoing mystery.

- It is generally agreed that the fastest period of brain growth is in the first four years or so of life, with the growth in the first year to 18 months perhaps being particularly dynamic.[9]

- The brain has time-related surges in development which roughly correspond with periods of significant shifts in skills and abilities.[10] The early years contain a number of these surges, with another significant 'wave' occurring in adolescence.

- The brain itself is a product of millennia of evolution in humans, just as in other mammals, and so many of its basic structures and allied functions are similar to those of other species.

- Contrary to some earlier perspectives on brain development, *'new neural connections in response to experience can be made across the lifespan'*.[11] In other words, we can adapt and change ways of thinking and behaviour over time.

- The brain has areas of specialisation which appear to deal with different types of information such as vision, emotions, memory, learning, hearing, etc., but it is also an *associative* organ, bringing together and combining sensory and emotional information. This forms the 'complete picture' that we experience in our day-to-day lives.

- The human brain survives and builds on a continuous stream of information from both body and environment, but too much or too little information can cause stress in one form or another.

- At birth the brain is *'the most undifferentiated of any "organ" in the body'*.[12]

- The right hemisphere is more advanced than the left from about the 25th gestational week until around early into the second year of life.[13] It is also the right side of the brain which appears to be intimately involved in processing the emotional and sensory information the baby encounters and the responsive outcome.

- While our genetic inheritance provides the information for the brain's structure, function and how it grows and matures, it is *experience* which ultimately influences the way in which the brain is uniquely 'wired' for each individual. As LeDoux puts it, *'nature and nurture are partners in our emotional life'*.[14] This point links with the information above, i.e. that our understanding of the world is unique to each of us.

- Areas in the brain that mediate what are termed 'executive functions' – i.e. planning, organising, self-monitoring, problem solving and sequencing – mature much later than those areas of the brain that process our more fundamental functions and our emotions.
- The newborn baby's brain already has a *'uniquely complex anatomy with all major systems present in various stages of immaturity'*.[15]

The human brain is a combination of genetic information in the way it builds up from the beginning of life and the way in which the various parts are organised. As can be seen from the points above, it is our *experiences* which 'fine tune' the connections between the various areas of the brain. Basically, our brains are all the same, and at the same time are uniquely different. Like an orchestra tuning up for the full concert, the hundred billion brain cells we are born with and the basic connections that have already been made because of the infant's activity and experiences in the womb are ready and waiting for the experiences which will constitute the symphony that will be the unique child.

One of the oldest parts of the brain, and the earliest to develop in the womb, is the brain stem; this is involved with evolutionary safeguards against danger, i.e. the newborn baby will usually show a 'startle' reflex and begin to cry if feeling unsafe or placed alone on a cold surface. This response to a possible threat to survival is therefore entrenched in the human brain at its very oldest and deepest level. Another ancient part of the brain and one which, like the brain stem, we share with other creatures, is the interconnected structures which form part of what is termed the 'limbic' or 'emotional' brain, which drapes around the brain stem in a semblance of a rim (hence the name). This part of the brain over long periods of time becomes more intertwined with what can be termed the 'thinking' or 'logical' brain. However, we have to be aware that the strong connections between these parts of the brain are very much a two-way process, and as we know, our emotions can frequently override logic.

An important structure within this 'emotional' brain is called the 'amygdala'; this tiny area has strong connections with memory, the production of bodily chemicals, the 'logical' part of the brain, the senses and also with the ancient brain stem. It has been shown to be particularly involved with fear and anxiety. Cozolino tells us that the amygdala has already reached a *'high degree of maturity by the eighth month of gestation, allowing it to associate a fear response to a stimulus prior to birth'*.[16] Linking this information with its further development at birth and its role in the assessment of danger, responses and emotions, there is a strong indication that the baby is already 'primed' for awareness of threat in any form;

hence a baby and very young child's strong reaction to something they think of as dangerous in any way. We also have to remember that what frightens a baby or child or appears 'dangerous', may seem very ordinary to us, for example, having a hair cut.

Babies are exquisitely sensitive to the expressions on faces, and this reaction appears to be 'hard-wired' into the human brain. This helps to explain why babies can respond so quickly to faces that seem angry or sad, as well as those that seem happy or contented. Also, these parts of the brain have links with those areas that speed up or slow down our heart rate, breathing, and also our digestion. I wonder how many of you feel 'butterflies' in the stomach when you are anxious or have a really strong need to go to the toilet. This helps us understand how what we term our emotions are so strongly linked with what we feel in our bodies; think about the lump in the throat, for example, or how we use bodily terms to identify what we find troubling. For example, 'she is such a pain in the neck', 'it feels like I am carrying the world on my shoulders', 'he is blind to what she is doing to him' and so on. Again, these structures are also involved in the production of the hormones in response to stressful situations, which links with the opening to this chapter. In other words, from the beginning of life, we react with brain and body to our experiences and we also lay down a memory in response to those experiences. It is on these earliest sensory memories that we base the reactions of our later life. Overall, it is the limbic system which appears to act as both filter and coordinator of the streams of information coming both from our bodies and all that sensory information from the external environment.

All this helps us understand that when a school-age child reacts to something that seems threatening in some way to them, those ancient, neurological systems will swing into action and, because of the immaturity of their brains, they will have only the earliest beginnings of the ability to 'rationalise' the reality or otherwise of the possible threat they encounter.

In evolutionary terms the newest part of the brain is the cortex. The very front part of the cortex is also the slowest to develop and it is this frontal cortex which appears to deal with the most abstract and complex of brain functions, e.g. thinking, planning and understanding, and with the recognition of what we are feeling, i.e. 'I know I am sad'. The very front of this front part, unsurprisingly called the prefrontal cortex, comprises about 29 per cent of the total cortex in humans compared to, for example, 7 per cent in dogs. This gives us an idea as to how important this part of the brain is. It seems to be very involved with how we manage our emotions. The prefrontal cortex is described by Goldberg as *'probably the best connected part of the brain'* and seems to be directly interconnected with every important structure within that limbic system.[17]

Another area of the cortex appears to be involved with movement, where we are in space and also our body image. Another important area, which is just above and behind our ears, deals with hearing, language, comprehension, sound and some aspects of memory and emotion. The back of this part of the brain seems to be mainly occupied with processing vision.

If we link our understanding that experiences shape the brain through the way in which experience forges those connections between all the different parts of the brain with the fact that our more logical brain is much slower to develop than our ancient emotion systems, we can see that the way in which emotions are dealt with by parents/carers will influence the strength and manner of how we learn to manage our emotions/behaviour.[18] Children have *to learn* to manage their behaviour in all the situations in which they find themselves. It can be seen that children need strong support in order to be able to do this. Without such help children may grow but not 'grow up' as Perry puts it.[19]

The cortex is divided into two and these halves are not absolute mirror images of each other. There are also some biochemical differences, with receptors for some neurochemicals being more prevalent in one hemisphere than another.

What is also of note is that the right and left sides of the brain appear to have different but complementary functions, so while structures on the right and left side are broadly reflective of each other, their 'focus of attention' can be slightly different. Overall, the right hemisphere appears to be biased towards emotional processing (especially sadness), self-awareness, facial recognition, bonding/ attachment and the big picture, while the left appears to be more biased towards facts, analysis, awareness of others and is generally more cheery![20]

What we also need to consider when thinking about helping children learn is some awareness of growth spurts within the brain, with the right side of the brain being more dominant in the first 18 months to two years, with the left hemisphere showing a growth spurt starting around the end of this period, incidentally tying in with a surge in verbal language development. These alternating growth spurts continue until approximately puberty, when the brain undergoes a period of great re-organisation, when growth spurts, chemical changes – e.g. in sleeping patterns and emotional shifts – and changes all occur. These alternating periods may help us think about what *types* of learning may be the general focus for the developmental needs of the child. For example, Siegal considers that *'the period between 3 and 7 years of age appears to be a profoundly important time for the acquisition of executive attentional functions raising the notion that interventions may be best initiated at this time'*.[21] It is interesting to note that this suggestion reinforces the idea that children are beginning to be able to shift their focus of attention from themselves to others with growing (but still very early and vulnerable) understanding of the different thoughts and needs of others during this period.

It is important to emphasise that pathways or systems within the brain are developed in response to the child's emotional environment so that a child who is nurtured, protected, loved, talked to and played with will develop circuits which lay a foundation for well-being and emotional health. It is true, as Gerhardt put it, that love certainly does matter.[22]

There is another piece of information about the brain, or rather its structures, which is also important; it is about the cerebellum, which lies behind the brain stem, appears to have its own unique organisation and is densely packed with brain cells. Its function appears to be associated with short-term memory, learning new skills, spatial awareness and sequencing, in addition to its long-established association with motor development and control. This latter is particularly important given the growing understanding of how movement influences learning.[23]

At birth it is large and very immature, with development occurring mainly after birth, the fastest period of growth being between birth and 15 months and generally with a *faster rate than the cortex'* between birth and four years of age. Studies by Knickmeyer *et al.* point to a growth in its volume of *240 per cent* in

Figure 1.1 *It is true, as Gerhardt put it, that love certainly does matter*

the first year, which may reflect the rapid growth in the motor abilities and balance of the baby during this time.[24] Maturation appears to continue at a much slower rate until around 15 years, which is unsurprising as motor abilities, etc. go through a profound change during puberty.[25]

One of the most fascinating developments in recent years to support our understanding of the brain (which is still, in reality, in its infancy) is the new technology that allows researchers and scientists to examine pictures of the living brain. This is giving support for both the existence of *broadly* specialised areas in the brain for various functions. Also, that children and adults may use different areas for the same task, which reinforces a role for the slow process of brain maturation and the accompanying role of experience.[26] Emotions are also interactive with brain maturation, as well as language, cognitive skills, movement and control over bodily functions. At only a few hours old, babies will respond differently to happy, sad or surprised faces, and are able to display facial, vocal and bodily signs of general contentment and distress which over the first year become more differentiated into joy, sadness, anger, fear and disgust.[27] More sophisticated emotions such as embarrassment and shame are thought to enter the emotional stage at around 14 months, tying in with the beginnings of a sense of ownership of body awareness and represented through the strong feelings evoked in children of this age by the ideas of 'me' and 'mine', which explains why children find 'sharing' so difficult!

The importance of the senses

When we consider the behaviour of children, including their capacity to learn, we need to think about how they are actually experiencing their world at a sensory level. Children do provide clues in their attitudes and behaviour towards different types of stimuli. For example, what are our favourite foods and how much does the texture influence what we like to eat. If you are a fan of crisps, you may not only enjoy the taste, but also the crispy texture and the sound of the crunching (not so popular in a cinema!). If you hate rice pudding, it may be that you feel this particular food is 'slimy'. I have a friend who hates mashed potato just because she cannot stand the softness of it! These are not just adult foibles, as parents know only too well; likes and dislikes are linked to our sensory experience of what we taste, see, feel and touch, as well as what we experience when we move our bodies. Such responses and sensitivities will influence how we approach new experiences. A teacher who wears perfume may wear the very one that a child may love or hate, and this will influence how that child approaches the teacher. These sensitivities begin at, and possibly before, birth with the baby who is 'bomb proof' to the one who startles at the slightest noise, or who is sensitive to heat or cold or the whisper of a draught or the sound of something being dropped in the kitchen.

Overall, the senses within the brain are all composed of the same electrical impulses, but are ultimately experienced rather magically both as individual senses – we know what we see, hear and feel, etc. as discrete entities – and as a rich combination of our senses. For example, if we think of the example at the beginning of this book, we experience the sea shore or the supermarket with all our senses. For the baby, some sensory systems are more involved than others, as smell and hearing are fully formed at birth (although not where a sound comes from for hearing); vision is minimal, but good enough to see faces; and taste is confined to the four basic taste experiences, i.e. sweet, sour, bitter and salt, although a fifth, 'umami', has also been discovered. Another sense that is fully formed at birth is that of the vestibular sense arising from the middle ear; this relates to body position and is important as the child grows. We also, of course, get lots of sensory information from within our bodies, which also influences how we experience and respond to the world.

For example, how a parent responds to the baby or child's behaviour will provide a scaffold for how the child will then organise their responses/behaviour, and this in turn will influence the ongoing adult response. This is just as true for teachers and other practitioners. The child will respond to approaches based on their prior experiences and the adult will respond accordingly. Remember the example of the perfume; but also the quiet child may be overwhelmed by an exuberant teacher or be dismayed at a distant greeting. We are what we know and we know what we experience. Sometimes the reality of our behaviour is as simple and as complex as that.

Summary: the melody lingers on

This chapter has set out to explain about how our brains work, with the emphasis on the realisation that early experiences lay down connections between all the different parts of the brain which subsequent experience can modify but *never totally eradicates*. The senses, too, linked together by both experience and our emotional responses, provide the main scaffold for how we build our sense of self and our view of the world. This is common to all human beings. Culture and social class, education, faith, etc. all come into play, but these influence more the *expression* of emotion rather than whether we feel or don't feel. Our brains follow the same construction, as does the way our bodies develop from the top down and the inside to the outer. In order to understand others, we have to learn about ourselves. In the next chapter we look at play and how this helps us manage this important part of growing up and learning.

Challenges and dilemmas

- Practitioners need to develop the skill of presenting learning to children in ways that can be processed by the young mind. Having too much or too little information causes stress to the child.
- Key people should recognise that although all areas of development inter-link, in the young child the emotional aspect is crucial in driving other areas of development such as self-awareness, trust, empathy and high self-esteem.

CHAPTER 2

Play, imitation and exploration; development's instrument

In the preceding chapter, I talked about development being somewhat like a three-part harmony, with the brain and the senses providing one strand of this melody. I think about the importance of play as somehow being the instrument on which this melody is played. I hope this doesn't seem too fanciful, but without play, in all its different forms, the full symphony of the child's development would not be realised.

This chapter therefore talks about how play and playful experiences engage children in their discovery of themselves and the world around them; how play enables children to come to new understandings in safe, yet challenging ways. In addition, this chapter will consider imitation, which is a fundamental part of human behaviour, providing a platform for early experiences on which more complex play and learning can then develop over time.

The developmental role of play

When we think about play, it is important that we realise there are strong links between play and the overall shifts in development as the child grows older. For example, the type of play that a baby will engage in is so different from the complex and sophisticated play you may have observed in a three-year-old or the rule-based play that a six-year-old will happily enjoy. However, no matter the age of the child nor the type of play, there is a two-way process occurring. That is, as the child plays, the child is learning, and as the child learns there is an impact on development, such as the child's ability to persevere and focus. These, in turn, are bound up with the child's emotions, behaviour and general communication skills. Children who are unhappy, anxious or frightened in some way will tend to either not play freely or become involved in play that is somewhat 'mechanical' and/or repetitive. This is true for animals, too; those in distress will not play but, if you have access to the internet, watch a baby elephant play in the sea with a piece of seaweed and you will witness the joy in play and exploration of the environment. I remember some years ago, watching some chimpanzees playing in a pool of water which had formed in a sandy part of their enclosure.[1] They dug holes, scraped water into them and watched, fascinated, as the water 'disappeared'. My husband had to drag me away from watching! All animals play, but as I said earlier, those in distress do not and neither do babies and very young children. It also makes me wonder whether the same principle applies in much older children and teenagers so that, if anxious and/or troubled they find it extremely difficult to find any joy or interest in school-based activities (never mind the classroom!). This leads perhaps to the need to 'escape' by experimenting with alcohol and/or drugs or to become involved in destructive behaviour or their becoming obsessed with video gaming. The latter, to me, has links with the mechanical and rather repetitive play of the sad and anxious child.

However, to turn back to the baby and very young child, these reflections on play lead on to thinking that because of the very nature of play and how it

Figure 2.1 *There is something absolutely fundamental about what play means to the child*

seems to be an essential part of the development of human and animal young, there is something absolutely fundamental about what play means to the child. This suggests how important it is that practitioners need to recognise how much they can learn by observing children at play. For example, *how* the child plays can provide not only some insight into the levels at which the child is actually functioning, which can be *very* different from the child's chronological age, but also what aspects of their personality and temperament they bring to their play. Do they, for example, show curiosity, persistence or enjoyment?

As part of my research into the quality of play with a group of children with autism and a group with learning difficulties, I discovered that the level of play in children with autism, in particular, was very different from that suggested by their competence level assessed by more formal methods. This leads me to wonder whether the approach that practitioners use to involve and engage them is actually truly 'age appropriate' for them.

For all early years practitioners, no matter what their role, play is a rich source for observation and learning about the child's world. It is so important, in fact, that 'play' should never be undermined and opportunities for play and exploration should not be seen as some sort of 'time filler', but as an integral part of the child's day. This ensures that children can develop their capacity for play, too, and become confident in exploring their surroundings, finding out what things are, what they do and how they can develop their understanding. All the time that this is happening, of course, the child will be learning about interactions, as well as learning what they want or are able to do by themselves. Because of the potential richness of the information provided by watching children at play, whatever their age and context, it saddens me that such observations of children are not more used as a means of truly understanding how well or otherwise a child may be understanding their world and the people within it.

Before moving on to the different types of play, I want to mention here one particular aspect of playful activity which also has an important role; that of imitation. This is because imitation has a powerful part in human behaviour from babies to adults, at which stage imitation becomes much more subtle but no less important. For example, have you noticed how people who are very close emotionally often, without realising it, imitate one another's body language? They become a reflection of one another. Parents, again almost instinctively, imitate the mouth movements, expression and body movements of their baby, and so the baby gets feedback through what they both physically and emotionally feel from the facial expressions they are seeing. For example, the parent saying 'give us a smile' is said with a broad smile on their own face, and if the baby responds with their own smile, then the parent's delight and much wider smile, head nodding and eye widening provides a huge response to the baby, who then smiles even more. The baby not only gets the sensations of its own face, but also what this wonderful experience *feels* like and so the baby will express its joy further through lots of arm waving, kicking and so on; just lovely! However, not only is this delightful for parent and child, the baby is getting a powerful lesson in how we as humans express our pleasure and happiness, all through the wonderful art of imitation in a playful context. This strongly suggests that the capacity to imitate is essential for human development, and as imitation in the early months is often in the context of play, and as play crosses species boundaries, playfulness itself is probably also an innate and essential component of development, thereby further establishing the capacity for play as an area for observation.

If we think about this further, we can begin to see how playful imitation of the baby's own actions and expressions, together with playful activities such as gentle tickling, rocking, bouncing, bringing the baby's attention to other people, toys, pets stimuli, begin to organise the baby's experiences so that different repeated actions become associated with their individual sensations and feelings. In other words, parents, carers and practitioners almost intuitively use imitation and play, in tandem with nurturing activities, to establish contact with their babies. These activities are intended to amuse, which in turn helps promote curiosity and exploration in the baby. Such interactions, together with the accompanying mutual smiling and laughter, provide an emotional context heavily weighted towards the positive; such play is also often in the context of nurturing and caring activities such as feeding, bathing and nappy changing. Many mothers will smile at, talk to or sing to their babies while feeding and blowing 'raspberries' on a baby's tummy is often a fun part of nappy changing! It can be seen that much of the baby's experiences are aimed at promoting contentment and reducing any distress or discomfort.

The different forms of play

One of the earliest types of play is that generally known as 'object play', which is the type of play that can be observed in babies and very young children, and also in the examples mentioned earlier: the baby elephant with his piece of seaweed and the chimps with the water and sand. This play is all about '*what can I do with this*' and leads to much exploration in babies: banging, mouthing, feeling, etc. However, an earlier question is '*what is it?*' and such exploratory or 'heuristic' play helps to combine both the 'what is it?' question and the 'what can I do with it?'. 'Heuristic play' is defined in the *Oxford Dictionary* as '*a system of education under which the pupil is trained to find out things for himself*'.[2] For example, watch a baby exploring a wooden spoon. The baby is finding out about texture, weight, shape and what it might taste like (not very nice, probably). The baby waving it about may then suddenly discover that something can be scooped with it or will be shown by an adult who may mime eating from it what might be its use; the adult will probably also name the object so the baby can slowly begin to link that this particular type of thing also has a name. Incidentally, the baby learns its own name during all the daily activities (and also the name of any pets), so the fact that people and animals have names and also that items in their environment have names allows this deep knowledge about their world to begin.

As said earlier, this early type of exploration combines the '*what is it?*' and '*what can it do?*' questions; when you observe an older child rolling a car along the floor, loading toy bricks into a truck or making a complex structure with different sized blocks, this is taking the play a little further as '*what can I do?*' becomes more complex. The development into a more complex type of exploration is supported when children have resources with which they can build, take apart and rebuild, which is why bricks are so wonderful; all that building up and knocking down!

Another type of play which will certainly be observed and is common to humans and animals is locomotor play, which as its name suggests is to do with locomotion or movement. Locomotor play, therefore, means all those wonderful leaps, jumps, twists, somersaults, chasing and rolling that are involved. Of course, dance includes all these movements, inspired initially by this type of play, and so a child dancing to music is also extending their repertoire of movement. Just think of some of the moves in the popular TV show *Strictly Come Dancing* and think about the children you will have observed spinning, standing on one leg (a late and complex movement), rolling, etc. Gymnasts, too, will display marvellous skills, but without the opportunity for free movement I doubt if their innate potential would be realised. Such play has a developmental purpose of course, and some researchers have suggested that in animals leaping helps animals to learn about the types of ground they have to negotiate. This applies to humans, too, because once a child is able to walk they need to learn to walk on different types of ground, as well as learning where it is safe to walk and run. This type of play also helps the child's balance, as swinging upside down helps the child learn about where they are in space, as does spinning. Simply putting one foot in front of the other requires good balance. Just try standing with one foot in front of the other (without turning either foot slightly outwards) and see how hard it is to keep the feet straight without wobbling. Incidentally, research linking brain development and play in mice shows a clear relationship between play and the growth of connections in the cerebellum, thus providing a link in how play supports quality of movement. Orr notes how children with physical disabilities are far less likely to be involved with, or encouraged, to take part in movement, which is why in many special schools there are opportunities for rolling, sliding and supported physical play, including dance, no matter how limited.[3]

We must not forget the social aspect of such locomotor play. I have mentioned in previous works that Nishida includes a category of social locomotor play in animals which seems to be similar to rough and tumble in children. He describes a young chimpanzee *'climbing a tree, followed by one or more youngsters, hanging . . . and falling or leaping down to the ground. . . . They repeat the entire sequence again and again.'*[4] The element of imitation is strong and I'm sure many practitioners have witnessed exactly the same type of play in human children. Sadly, especially in view of the seminal work by, who stresses the importance of *'rough and tumble play'* and describes it as the *'brain sources of joy'*, such type of play is sometimes seen as aggressive or too rough and stopped.[5] For many boys particularly, and I make absolutely no apology for this generalisation, such play is an important part of their development; fundamentally learning how strong (or weak) they are in relation to their peers and also learning about how far to go in such play. This latter aspect is also noted again in animal research with animals learning when and how to use their strength and adapt their play in order not to hurt a weaker member of the group. As an example, I have watched my dogs at play; the younger one would adapt his behaviour so that the older one did not have to run around quite so much while the older one, who was also much heavier, appeared to instinctively avoid rolling onto his playmate when they were both tussling on the ground.

This same-sex play occurs in older children (around about 6–7 years) and perhaps points to its importance in helping social and physical skills in each gender. Many girls tend not to be involved in the same type of physical play, but certainly do enjoy dance and/or balancing and swinging. Skipping also seems (or seemed) to be an activity which appeals to girls, as well as games such as 'hopscotch', which is wonderful for balance. Girls at this age also seem to enjoy playing with other girls rather than in mixed groups, and perhaps this also points to the importance of allowing children to play as they choose. Each gender may have a particular way of framing their social locomotor play, with neither type being more negative or positive than the other but instead being a crucial part of development for both.

Perhaps the most sophisticated and complex manifestation of play is when children begin to be able to pretend and imagine, which, incidentally, also supports the later development of reading and writing because being able to imagine means that a child is capable of understanding that you can see something 'in your head', which more formally can be described as the ability to under-stand symbolic representation. At this point I would like to consider what skills and abilities *precede* the emergence of the more complex fantasy/imaginative/role play. What is fascinating is that these skills and abilities all occur within a similar developmental time frame, building up a wonderful jigsaw which when put together seems to enable the child to play in increasingly complex ways. The time frame within which these abilities gradually develop is within the second year of life. However, we must remember that no ability, just like beha-viour, simply happens, but builds on those learning experiences, emotional, social interactions, communication and physical development which have already occurred. We must also remember that it is the quality and consistency of all these experiences which will influence the way in which these new abil-ities actually develop. The child who is hardly ever spoken to (except perhaps to be shouted at) will have a different level of the following types of develop-ment, for example, than a child who is noticed, cared about, talked to and played with.

Within the second year, then, we are likely to notice the following:

- understanding likes and dislikes such as different tastes, the feel of some clothes, etc.
- the beginnings of understanding another's feelings, such as offering a sad child a toy
- a surge in the levels of imitation by children of adult actions, as well as a means of communication between each other. Watch children watching others to see what they do
- an emergence of understanding goal-directed actions; in other words a child can begin to understand what the adult wants them to do and can follow very simple instructions
- an emergence of verbal communication
- a greater awareness of the self as a self, e.g. recognition of the self in a mirror.

In addition, for a child to be able to pretend, there has to be an understand-ing of the properties of objects in the real world, their reliability and consist-ency in lots of different situations; as with everything, such knowledge begins in the very earliest days of life. For example, the child has (hopefully) learned that certain faces, scents and types of touch are reliably associated with the carers in their life and, of course, playful interactions as well as nurture has helped these pictures of the adults and others around them to develop. Being given the opportunity to touch, feel, smell, taste and explore their world has also helped them to gradually understand (over several months) that something out of sight can still exist and then gradually realise that an object can be moved, and found, in a different place. So when adults play 'peek a boo' with a baby they are instinctively helping the baby learn that something can appear and disappear and be the same thing and then, when adults hide objects and produce them again, all this helps to learn these truly fundamental ideas about the world. Can you imagine what it would be like if we were unsure of the hardness of a table and had to discover it every time? So when you think about a child's ability to pretend, they certainly would not be able to imagine a wooden brick as a cake if they were uncertain as to the properties of both a brick and a cake. They know that a brick is not a cake, but they can pretend it is; and pretend to eat it.

However, there is much pretending that appears to be an intermediate state between imitation and more complex representation, i.e. substituting one thing for another and that is when the child uses a real phone to pretend to talk to a parent or friend or pretends to go to sleep during a play situation by lying down and closing their eyes.

What we usually understand as pretend play in children means that they use toys and play materials in order to extend play and also allows for one thing to represent another – literally *re*-presenting. What is fascinating in such young children is that they don't get confused when playing pretend and being in the real world, but instead seem to be able to move back and forth between these two worlds without any problem. In 1987 Alan Leslie wrote a seminal paper on 'Pretense and Representation'[6] and he dwelt on just this fact. He put forward a theory that children can somehow *'decouple'* these experiences and he also put forward three questions he said could identify whether a child is actually pretending or simply imitating adult's actions with props and that any one of these aspects can indicate pretence. These are:

- Has one object been made to stand for another, such as a brick for a cake or a stick for a wand?
- Has a pretend property been attributed to an object or situation? Leslie's example is if a child says that their dolly's (clean) face is dirty.
- Has a child said that an object is there when it is not, e.g. there's milk in an empty jug that the child then 'pours'.

It is interesting to think about the levels of pretend play. If a child pretends to eat a plastic piece of fruit, this is still pretend but at an earlier or simpler level than if the child pretends to eat the brick pretending it's a cake. This is because while the child knows that the plastic apple is not real and therefore only pretends to eat it, at the same time, the plastic apple is something that the child knows is representing something that the child can really eat. It is this simpler representation that can be termed 'concrete' play, whereby the child uses replicas of real objects to support pretence, e.g. a toy tea set, a doll, small-world toys. Such items can, of course, become part of fantasy play too, as when a child uses them as props in an elaborate story where the toy animals have characters, different voices and adventures.

Throughout their early months and years, children have been watching and observing adults, what they do in different situations, how they greet people, what happens at meal times and so on. This all means that children, through this extensive imitation and observation of daily activities, can then move onto their own conscious form of *as if*. For example, I am stirring a spoon in an empty pot *as if* there was something in the pot to stir.

Another wonderful aspect of pretend play is that children seem able to understand when another child is pretending and will join in the game, such as playing pirates or being princesses, with hardly any props at all. The ships and the swords or the crowns and dresses are simply in the minds of the children, with perfect understanding between them; invisible and yet seen clearly in the mind's eye. Leslie and other researchers have wondered why, when children are able to do this, it takes so long for them to understand that someone can know something different to them; what is termed a 'false belief'. The famous example that is often given is that a child can be shown a tube of sweets and be asked what is in it. The child will logically say *'sweets'*. When the case is opened, the child sees that there are no sweets, but rather boring pencils. They are then asked if someone came into the room and saw the tube, what might they think was inside. It takes most children up to and a little beyond four years of age before they will reliably say *'sweets'*. Up until that time they will say *'pencils'* as this is what *they* know is in the tube. While this puzzled Leslie, I wonder if it is simply that perhaps the child needs to practice through pretend play different roles and ideas and so gradually the child can begin to comprehend the complexities of understanding that one individual can have different knowledge to someone else.

To return to imagination, another facet of pretend play that appears to support a growing understanding of someone else's mind is the child's enthusiasm for taking on the role of someone else. In imaginative play, children imitate the common phrases, behaviours and attitudes of the adults in their family (much to their dismay at times!) and it is from this that they can move on to add their own 'twist' to the situations as their play becomes more self-determined and wider in context, embracing more characters and situations. What you may have noticed of the average three-year-old is that their thinking is strongly, and rightly, focused on working out the self; building on the realisation of being a 'self' and the determined nature of the two-year-old. However, the other gift that the opportunities for fantasy and role play provide is that as they take on the different roles of doctor and nurse, baby and parent, dog and other pets, princess and superman, bus conductor and traveller; all these and the other roles that they take will allow the child to move out of themselves in a way and try out another way of being. It is an extension of the de-coupling of real and imaginary objects to an abstract version of this process. I strongly suggest that imaginative play of this type is a *necessary* prerequisite to the capacity to understand the minds and thoughts as well as the feelings of others, and so delay, dysfunction or lack of opportunity in this area can potentially disrupt the quality and perhaps extent of this fundamental ability.

We have to remember that play, at whatever level, also involves how the child is feeling. In the wonderful book by Panksepp, based on years of research, he emphasises that play is a *'primary emotional function of the mammalian brain'* and this is logical considering its presence and persistence across species. He notes that play must be enjoyable, otherwise no species would do it, plus the fact that emotions such as fear, as well as hunger, in animals *'can temporarily eliminate play'*. For example, young chimpanzees *'after several days of isolation ... become despondent and are likely to exhibit relatively little play when reunited'*. Comparisons can be found with the diminished capacity for play in human children when upset and/or fearful.[7]

These findings and a wealth of other animal research quoted by Panksepp stress that the capacity to play appears to rest on a basis of a warm and secure environment with abundant parental involvement and, of course, that of other adult carers. While adults should not take over play, they certainly need to be sensitive and aware of the play that is occurring and provide support as and when necessary. This is a truly important skill!

Links with language

Harris[8] discusses language and imagination extensively and describes how the emergence of language in tandem with the emergence of pretend play builds on the child's ability to create a model of a situation which, the author suggests, they have practised through imitation of adult actions. During such play children can produce language that includes what they have done and what they are about to do, allowing the mind to move between past, present and future and so, of course, helping the child begin to understand about time. The situations that children will often re-enact are situations that they, as children, have experienced and so also experience a narrative that flows in time. They are helped of course by story telling, and especially fairy stories, which traditionally begin *'Once upon a time'* and end with *'They lived happily ever after'*, bringing in something that does not exist in the present time but once (past) and which will be (future). Fairy stories also often allow children's basic fears to be addressed safely and with a positive resolution. It is a shame that traditional stories can be seen by some as somehow not politically correct, when in fact many cultures have similar tales. The wisdom of the past, which recognises that children do have fears which need to be dealt with appropriately, can be lost. Children also need to understand the flow within a story and within their play so that they can then understand their own autobiography and links can be made between the growing ability to recall more about past events which occurs around this time, with the surge in language development and the opportunity for practice in all these skills that children are getting in play. The huge concern with the development of literacy and concerns about reading levels in children illustrates how knowledge and understanding of what supports literacy is also crucial for practitioners supporting children.

To sum up

Playing imaginatively is possibly one of the most interesting and complex aspects of the capacity to play. Children move from being 'in the now' to not only elaborating and extending their day-to-day experience, but entering worlds that they can create. It provides an opportunity for them to 'try out' their capabilities – and especially to learn that they can have some control of what they do and how. They set the scene of the pirate ship or the fairy castle or the dog kennel and work out who will play what role, perhaps to take charge and/or to learn the beginnings of negotiation and to deal with the frustration when others don't want to take a particular role. How rich indeed and how necessary for the emotional growth and well-being of a child! Play in all its various forms allows for the 'practice' of how to be with other people, of learning about themselves and widening the boundaries of their experience.

Finally, what is absolutely crucial is that children, whatever their age, are given developmentally appropriate play materials and, of course, the opportunity to playfully explore their world. This can be through their own initiated play or with the support of adults who may tell a story which then captures the imagination of the children who then act out and develop the themes within the story.

It must be recognised, too, that children do not need extensive (and expensive) props in order to play. Opportunities outdoors to explore leaves and twigs can turn into magical stories; to splash in puddles helps find out about water and wetness (and the lovely comfort of getting dry; transition). Role play areas need to have some static elements, however, because children also, paradoxically perhaps, need some routine and consistency so they feel safe enough to let their minds run free. Changing the role play area or not leaving some basic props there, such as soft toys, pans, some bowls, blankets, boxes of different sizes and hats which can all be lovingly used over and over again in a variety of contexts, can be distressing and confusing for many children.

So much can and is learned through play; about the child themselves, the people around them and their particular world. Children will play in the most impoverished conditions, and so for the sake of all children: let them play!

Challenges and dilemmas

- Recognising that play is a two-way process; as a child plays, they learn; and this learning impacts on their type and levels of play. Bruner's spiral curriculum demonstrates this interaction between play and development.
- For children to develop effectively, play needs to offer rich learning experiences. In this way children will display the characteristics of effective learning such as curiosity, persistence and enjoyment.

Learning to be secure, learning to learn and the nurturing practitioner

This chapter aims to help practitioners understand the ways in which children may approach or withdraw from learning opportunities. It will consider the fundamental need for a child to feel emotionally as well as physically safe in their environment. I want to reflect on how a child's early experiences will influence their particular behaviour towards different people and different situations. This will hopefully allow you, as practitioners, to think with compassionate understanding about the children in your care. The children you meet will display a range of different types of behaviour, including those who may have difficulty becoming involved or appear to withdraw from support or be consumed with anxiety. A really important point to remember is that no behaviour arises out of nothing; there are always reasons for why all of us, including children and those who care for them, behave as we do.

Linking what we do to how we feel

Any child's ability to concentrate and persist in an activity is fundamentally related to how they feel about that activity; just think about your own reactions to something you want or don't want to do. Are you eager, interested, pleased, or are you feeling reluctant and fearful you might not cope? Just like you, a child's reactions will depend on their experiences and the attitudes of the people within their environment towards them. While we can often be very aware of our own feelings towards whatever we have to do in our daily lives, I sometimes wonder whether we think enough about how a child may be feeling about the situations in which we put them? This does not mean, I hasten to add, that we simply 'go along with' whatever the child may appear to want to do. What I am saying is that we need to fully understand that reactions are built on experiences and even a very young child has had a multitude of positive and possibly negative experiences, all of which build towards the overall character of the child. By this I mean how the child appears to you, how they behave and respond, how they react to other children and towards other adults, how they are when they are met by parents and other relatives or carers; what is it that they do? Working with children not only entails deep knowledge about development, but also an observant eye and a willingness to step beyond or outside our own responses and attitudes and think about what situations mean for the child. If we acknowledge that children, like us, respond to different situations with feelings, then it becomes possible to think about the best way to respond in a particular situation. For example, if we know that going outside is anxiety-provoking for some children, this means we have to think about why. Possible reasons could include that they find other children too boisterous or there are bigger children who share the same space. It also suggests that these children may need more time and appropriate support in order to learn that it is possible to have quiet play by themselves or with just another child or learn strategies to help them cope when feeling overwhelmed. Simply 'jollying along' a child may be the worst thing to do!

Practitioners need to be aware, reflective and confident in their own approach, and this also means that practitioners need to have some insight into their own fears, likes and dislikes, something I will talk more about later.

First steps on the road to becoming secure

In order to think about what factors contribute to a child's general behaviour, motivation and attitudes, the question we ask is: What provides the foundation on which such characteristics are based? One answer is our level of security, and from this we have to consider what this actually means because being or feeling secure has many dimensions, from the very profound emotional meaning to the physical sense of security; of course, the former initially arises from the latter.

Perhaps one of the enduring myths about childhood is that we remember little or nothing about our experiences in the earliest months and years of our lives. Of course, there are always exceptions, with people remembering some particular incident in their infancy or toddlerhood and sometimes even their birth experience, but generally our recollection of those times appears to be either non-existent or at best sporadic. However, even though we may not apparently be able to recall our earliest years, it does not mean we do not remember; the key to this apparent contradiction lies in the fact that memory has many forms.

Types of memory

Essentially, we appear to have two types of memory, long term and short term, the latter more often called 'working' memory. Long-term memory itself is also divided into two types; the names for these are the explicit or declarative memory, and implicit or 'unconscious' memory, which includes procedural memory. Simply, what this means is that we have a long-term memory which allows us to talk about our past, and it is the type of memory which includes all those things that our brain processes without us being fully aware of it. Interestingly, in this type of memory, we can also include what is called 'procedural' memory, which is remembering how we do something. This is fascinating because even when people lose short- or long-term memory because of trauma or illness, they can often still learn a skill or remember how to tie a shoe lace, to knit or to sing the words of a well-known song. This ability helps us understand how someone with profound dementia, for example, can still respond and sing along to music they may have heard many times in their childhood, and indeed provides a way of reaching someone who may appear totally lost in their particular world. Although we may consciously make an effort to remember a dance step, play a game or drive a car, once we have learned such a skill it becomes automatic and we can then do other things at the same time. Just think about the effort a child puts into taking those first wobbly steps and how the whole body has to learn a new way of experiencing the world, i.e. standing up and moving forward so that one learns to avoid obstacles and balance adapts to enable walking on different surfaces. Now, reflect on the fact that you don't have to think about walking but simply do it automatically, and it is only if something happens that affects your limbs, muscles, balance or vision that you have to relearn how to put your foot forward. It is only when walking becomes a learned skill in the child (and therefore in their procedural memory) that they are able to do other things at the same time. Knowing about this helps us understand the apparent clumsiness of a child who may find walking difficult for one reason or another or why simply walking and carrying something can be such a huge effort for a child and require concentration and focus.

Before I move on I also want to mention 'working memory' and 'declarative' or implicit memory. These particular types of memory help us link the past with the present. Working memory holds the thread of our moment-to-moment experiences. The trauma which results in someone losing their working memory helps us understand the devastating effect of its loss. Without it we would be slaves to the moment as, for example, we would be unable to remember someone we had spoken to a short time before. Our experiences would always seem to be new ones.

Declarative or implicit memory is also divided into two: our autobiographical memory and our semantic memory. The latter is the one that deals with facts, such as the fact that London is the capital of England or Henry VIII had six wives. Autobiographical memory is just what it says – it is about us. It is also incredibly important in helping to identify a sense of self, that is, who we are, linking our past with the present and incidentally helping us think about the future. One fascinating link between memory and self is that our capacity to point to different parts of our body (at around 18 months or so) ties in with our ability to recognise ourselves in a mirror, and it also coincides with the emergence in many of us of language so that the knowledge of a physical body that 'belongs to me' also begins to be linked to a 'me to whom things happen which I can talk about'. In old age, or through trauma or disease, memory becomes affected; but not all the different types of memory, so elderly people may easily forget day-to-day occurrences (and those not so old!) but memories of childhood can be remembered with great clarity.

However, if working memory is lost, these memories can become confused in time and context so that the threads on which a coherent sense of the past and the present are based become tangled. That sense of self, too, can become increasingly blurred in profound dementia and sadly there seems to be a return to a very early child-like state but with the added complication of all those lifetime experiences swirling around in chaos as there is an unravelling of the links between experiences and emotions. This means that people may react in ways that seem unrelated to a particular happening within their day, but in their minds may link to something from the past, triggered by some common element in both the past and present circumstances. In such people, as with babies and very small children, familiar faces and routines help to ground their experiences and so lessen the anxiety in such adults and provide comfort and security for children.

Memory and the senses

The reason I have spent some time talking about memory and the different elements to it is that it helps us to realise that the baby and very young child remember at a deep, unconscious level all the experiences they have had from birth (and possibly before), and that those experiences are laid down in those early neural pathways talked about in Chapter 1. Memory is therefore not a single item but a multi-layered and complex system which, even now, is not fully understood. What we must remember about memory is that it is intimately tied in with our emotions, and it is what we feel about something that influences what we remember. It is important to realise that how we feel about a situation is influenced by the amount of sensory information that surrounds us. Sensory information is a mix of information from all the senses that are working and depends on the degree to which they are experienced. This means that if any particular sense is more sensitive or dull or absent, then it will influence the way such memories are laid down. It may be useful to mention here that practitioners need to think about the impact of the light in the room, smells (including their own perfume), sounds and the general feel of floors, furnishings, etc. when reflecting on the responses of children to activities. The general tidiness or untidiness or levels of cleanliness in the setting will also have an impact. Can you imagine what it might feel to a child to walk into a room where all seems chaos? Have you ever walked into a house or building where just the smell has put you off or found that a beautifully presented meal can help your appetite?

I just want to mention the impact of sensory information to how children may react at meal or snack times. As many practitioners know, eating together is wonderful for learning social skills, communication, eating habits and encouraging thinking about others. Sadly there seem to be many households where family meals appear to be minimal and so it is even more important that meal times in settings are given the importance they deserve. Incidentally, meal times also encourages number (counting how many forks, spoons, napkins, etc.) and matching (putting the cutlery with the plates, sorting out cutlery of different sizes); such a wealth of learning opportunities and yet so often these snack or meal times can be rushed. I remember watching with dismay when observing lunch in a setting, when the children's sandwiches were simply placed on the table, not even a paper plate was available. I wondered what lessons the children were learning about food in general, never mind the lack of interaction or opportunities for extending their learning through this social occasion. As many of you who may be fortunate enough to visit Europe will know, even the youngest children are involved in the family meal and quickly learn what is acceptable behaviour, as well as learning that they are part of the family group.

In light of all the above information, we can understand that we are surrounded by information from all our senses from birth, and this mix of information results in pleasant or unpleasant feelings. If something is pleasant it can catch our awareness and we may want to repeat that experience, and if we repeat it, we are more likely to remember it. Of course, a deeply unpleasant feeling will also be remembered because of the strength of its impact. In addition, we will try to avoid such feelings happening again by adopting all kinds of strategies to ensure the horrible feeling doesn't happen again; this, of course, gives us a hint as to why children and adults may behave in ways that seem inappropriate but which, in fact, have helped to avoid that particular feeling.

In adults the original experience which triggered the fear, anxiety or distress may be buried very deeply in their unconscious, but similarities to that experience in different circumstances can still produce echoes of that original distress and the resulting behaviour will also have echoes of how that experience was handled. As an example, I wonder if you have had experience of suddenly feeling very angry about something quite trivial that someone has said or done, or that saying 'no' to someone brings feelings of anxiety and distress? The origins of those feelings and responses may lie very deep in your own early experiences.

Learning to be secure

Nobody knows how babies understand the world around us, but what research tells us, and probably what most parents instinctively know, is that babies are certainly not without their own basic skills. Nature gives babies a head start through the existence of reflexes, including those of sucking and rooting and stepping, as well as the ones which relate to posture plus the hormonal, chemical rush that birth itself provides for both mother and baby. Babies even have some idea as to how objects are supposed to behave, and there is some wonderful research around (Robinson provides an overview[1]) which points to the notion that nature has given babies some initial ideas of how the world works. However, as I said, this is the head start or 'scaffold' that nature has put in place, but it is the responses and attitudes of the parents and carers of the baby that builds on this scaffold and profoundly influences the baby's slowly increasing understanding of itself and the world. Why these early experiences are so important is because a baby's world is very small and confined to those experiences which are orchestrated by adults. Therefore their early learning is centred around not only the type of relationship with their parents and carers, but also the levels of care and nurture they receive. In addition, their experiences will also encompass the characteristics of the particular environment in which they are living. The baby will experience the feel of their clothing, bedding, heat or cold, as well as noise from the sound of any pets and the interactions between other family members, the type of media within the home and so on. So the faces, sounds, smells, feel and taste of these highly consistent and persistent interactive experiences provide the foundations for what the world is actually like for the baby; whether positive or negative.

In the very first weeks it is often the experiences that the mother provides that shape the first glimmers of realisation that the baby is a unique individual. I realise that this is not a popular view in some quarters, but nature and evolution have worked together to provide mothers with skills that are essential for the well-being of the new baby. For example, women in general are far better at recognising the meaning of facial expressions and eye gaze than men and the vast majority of new mothers soon learn that their baby's expressions means something to them and they talk to their baby about how they are feeling and respond in ways that they feel appropriate. Mothers very quickly identify the different pitch and tone of their baby's cry as having different meanings; while fathers are also in tune with their babies, mothers seem to have the upper hand! When you think about it, this is nature's way of ensuring the baby's well-being. After all, babies are born in every situation all over the world and the first person they are going to have contact with is their mother, so nature does its best to ensure that mothers will want to hold and feed their baby and, of course, feeding provides a wonderful situation for closeness, physical contact and, so importantly, being able to gaze at one another. Alan Schore, writing in 1994[2] after many years of his own research and extensive review of other researchers' work concerning emotions and the effects on the early developing human brain, powerfully states the importance of this close interaction between mother and baby. Although this book was written in 1994, it remains one of the most powerful, extensive and comprehensive reviews of research into brain development and the role of emotions. To me, it registers something so crucial for emotional well-being in that the baby is truly seen. Unfortunately, neglect, and especially emotional neglect, which crosses all social classes, is itself ignored as a cause for unhappiness and unwanted behaviour. This is in spite of the impact of long-term emotional neglect on the mental well-being of the growing child and its effects which echo into adulthood in both overt and covert ways, such as finding difficulty in making and keeping relationships.

Fathers, of course, are very important and have caring and nurturing skills too, but in subtly different ways to mothers which are not really interchangeable. Schore considers that fathers really come into their own when the baby becomes a toddler.

Another example of how nature somehow prepares us for the inevitable life changes through the life span is that at around three months of age a baby begins to be less totally focused on their mother and increasingly attracted by other faces, sounds and so on. This can perhaps be the first step in the process of the baby being an individual (the baby starts to choose what to look at) but also brings in a degree of separation. This may seem fanciful, but how the mother deals with the baby not only being interested in her alone can be important. Some mothers find this shift in the baby's awareness quite painful – think about how parents feel when a child goes to nursery, then school, then perhaps work, college or university. Both parent and child have to deal with these partings (and ultimately the existence and experience of loss).

Figure 3.1 *The world is an exciting and sometimes scary place*

Understandably, sometimes parents can become extremely protective and while the child can seem able to cope fairly well – for example on the first day at nursery – the parent can be in pieces, something else a practitioner needs to understand.

The world is an exciting and sometimes scary place, but what is important for the child is that their emotions are anchored in the care and nurture of the parents and other carers who encourage but also keep the child safe, both physically and, just as importantly, emotionally.

Attachment

I am making an assumption here and also a hope that all practitioners working with children, whatever their discipline, will have received in their training information about attachment theory, although sadly there seems to be some variation in the levels of importance ascribed to it. This is the theory set out by John Bowlby,[3] particularly in his seminal works on attachment, separation and loss, which fundamentally address the issue of emotional security and how it comes about. There is a wealth of information on attachment theory in many texts and it is also one of the most well-researched theories across not only countries but also cultures. Bowlby became interested in developmental psychology when studying medicine at Cambridge University and, while working in a small residential unit, became interested in two children in particular. One followed him like a shadow, while the other was quiet and withdrawn. Both boys had disrupted childhoods and their experiences fed into Bowlby's thinking when he published his famous paper describing a study of adolescent criminals.[4]

Over time and with a combination of general dissatisfaction with the theories of the day plus his observations and the research of others regarding reactions to separation from mothers in both children and the animal kingdom, Bowlby slowly developed his theory of attachment. In particular, his work led him to believe that an infant's strong urge to be with their mother had evolutionary roots and could be observed in virtually all creatures, and that separation caused real distress.

Attachment theory is a theory of survival and a protection against danger. We need to learn that we have both a *safe haven* for comfort and a *safe base* for exploration. Ultimately, learning to feel safe and secure with our adult carer sets the scene for us to be able to carry that safe feeling *inside* us, helping us to feel confident in the way we go about our day-to-day business. Attachment theory, therefore, is one of the most viable ways of understanding not only children's reactions to separation and loss, but also their working capacities to manage emotions and relationships. So all practitioners, whatever their role or level of working, should understand the key principles of the theory. The point is that it really helps to understand the basis of a child's (and our) attitudes and behaviour, providing a degree of insight into the 'why' of behaviour, not just the 'what'. One of the most notable things about attachment theory is that neuroscientific research appears to substantiate the importance of positive emotional relationships in the earliest years in order to support healthy brain development and, in turn, the shaping of the child's developing personality.[5]

Danya Glaser[6] provides a very helpful resume in bringing out the key points of Bowlby's work. In particular, she emphasises his premise of the biological basis of attachment behaviour – that is, the seeking of proximity by a child to their carer in order to provide a secure base. She emphasises that this seeking, which is common in all young creatures, influences both emotions and behaviour and is caused by what she terms *'internal/external stressors'* which simply means feeling lost, lonely, afraid or being physically separated from the carer. I wonder if any of you have found yourself lost in a strange place or felt lonely – what did you feel would give you comfort? I imagine that some of you would wish your mother to be there or your father would come and rescue you and 'make it better' or you longed for the companionship of someone deeply loved? Perhaps, too, if feeling lonely, you found solace in stroking a pet or remember hugging your teddy bear or doll? Reflecting on the painful feelings such situations arouse may help us as adults show understanding when a child seems bereft at a separation or is distraught when told they can't have their teddy with them.

The great gift that Bowlby gave us was the idea that a child, any child, forms an attachment with their parent which is built on this biological search for safety; another of nature's starting points. Each child ideally needs a secure base from which they are able to explore their world with a degree of confidence. In particular, Bowlby talked about an 'internal working model' which is the model of their particular individual world. This model is helped in its construction by the type of relationship the child has with its main carers, embedded in all those sensory factors mentioned above. However, what Bowlby recognised, which was then explored by his colleague Mary Ainsworth, is that attachment relationships are not always secure by any means but can be insecure too. It may seem strange to think about an attachment as insecure because this need to be close to the parent or carer is so innate in a child. However, it is the responses of the adult, particularly to the child's distress, that provides the child with their first understandings of safety and security, inextricably bound up with how the child is generally feeling – for example, overall contentment versus general anxiety or fear or distress. Therefore, the type of attachment formed by the child towards its parent will influence their working model.

Research has shown that the quality of the attachment and its accompanying behaviour strategies can be reliably measured by the 'Strange Situation' at approximately one year of age. The Strange Situation is a process by which the quality of a child's attachment to its carers is formally assessed. It was devised by Bowlby's colleague Mary Ainsworth, and is carried out by specially trained practitioners. Adaptations of the initial format have been devised for assessment of older children, and for adults there is the Adult Attachment Interview devised by Mary Main, which again can only be carried out by practitioners who have successfully achieved the very specific training.

The echoes of those first attachment relationships do reach into adulthood, although changes in circumstances including alterations in how a parent responds to a child can alter the child's feelings of security. The effects of the primary attachments are not written in stone and can be modified and changed; nevertheless, the first attachment neural footprint does cast a long shadow.

This need to build an emotionally secure base is no less strong and just as necessary in those children who may have disabilities. Children with autism or any other special needs have parents who, like any other parent, will encompass the range of type and quality of care and responsiveness, and so the emotional environment of the child should not be neglected when considering behaviour. In principle there is no difference in the process of attachment formation in both typically and non-typically developing children.

As babies we begin to make an attachment relationship with our primary carer, who is usually our mother, from the moment we are born, and it is how this relationship develops over time that will establish the quality of the attachment relationship.

To summarise, the child's working model develops how they generally feel on a daily basis. All of us have mood swings dependent on our health, what is happening in our lives and so on, but there is also a kind of general undercurrent of emotion within all of us. Would you consider yourself to be mostly fairly contented, or are you anxious most of the time? Or perhaps you get angry or irritable very easily so that your general mood or feeling is one of being dissatisfied or frustrated. Are you somehow rather sad much of the time? Think about the children in your care or whom you mainly encounter in your work. How do they seem to you?

The working model will also affect children's general behaviour – in other words, babies and young children very soon develop a strategy to deal with their feelings which leads into how their model will affect the type of relationship the child has with you, and influence their tendency to approach new people or situations. This can be with curiosity and interest, wariness and disinterest or overexuberance, which can seem tinged with anxiety.

It is important to note that these strategies are formed before a child's conscious awareness of a bodily self, which again points to the profound nature of these early experiences. We need to learn to cope with our experiences from the beginning of our lives. Crucially, in the earliest months of life the adult is both the provider of the experiences and the arbiter in how this early coping begins, e.g. with reassurance, comfort, encouragement, pleasure and joy in their child, or intrusiveness, irritation, impatience, etc. Whatever it is, the child will reflect this in later life.

The nurturing practitioner

Children, and adults, cannot make close relationships with unlimited numbers of people; however, it is possible for a child to make close relationships with key figures in their lives. What all practitioners who work closely with children need to recognise is that they are attachment figures for those in their care. In other words, children will look to them for safety and security and, dependent on the child's particular needs, will develop a relationship of one kind or another. At the very least, the practitioner will provide an emotional and physical environment for every child which will have an impact on that child. I sometimes think the responsibility of those working in early years settings, childminders, those working in care homes and teachers have towards children is not always fully discussed. However, if practitioners have daily contact with children, then they do hold the child's heart and mind in their hands, so to speak. I am sure many of you can remember a teacher who made a huge impact on your attitudes towards a topic or to school itself for good or ill. I am eternally grateful to an English teacher who introduced me to a range of books which my parents, who were Italian immigrants, would possibly never have known about. She opened a whole world for me which allowed escape from my constant anxieties and insecurities, but that is another story. The point I want to strongly emphasise is that as practitioners, you matter to the child. Therefore what you do, how you behave and respond to the child's needs, and how you behave towards other adults, matters hugely. Children watch and learn all the time, even the very youngest, soaking up the emotional environment in which they are living. For those children who are lucky enough to have a loving and caring home, then a nurturing practitioner will add to and support the child's confidence and security. For the child who is not so fortunate, then the nurturing practitioner will open a new world to such a child; giving them a glimpse of different views and different ways of being. In other words, that the child is cared about. Such experiences provide a child with additional support, helping them increase their resilience to stressful situations. This is important because a sound relationship with key adults provides an anchor that children can use to help them cope with all the different situations adults provide. It may be useful for practitioners to think about how many transitions a child may have to contend with during a single day, both physically such as moving from one room to another, and emotionally such as dealing with different groups of children, different adults. Think about just how long a corridor may seem to a young child or how huge the playgroup can appear when they may have to cross from one side to another. Remember how large things seemed to you in childhood and perhaps when you revisited somewhere you lived or went to school how surprised you may be at the actual size of buildings or rooms. Also, I do sometimes also wonder how young children are meant to cope with all the adults involved in fractured families (never mind all the potential siblings and house moves).

As we have realised, from infancy children will develop strategies to deal with all the situations in which they find themselves and for those with confused, troubling or chaotic experiences. Their coping mechanisms may lead to potentially difficult behaviour. It is important that adults understand the limited capacity children have to deal with such situations and that the existence of solid, reliable adults is a key element in helping them cope and deal with their feelings. Sometimes it does seem as if we expect children to react with total calmness and acceptance to situations that as adults we recognise as being stressful.

So what does being a 'nurturing practitioner' mean? To me, it means that practitioners need to understand their role, responsibilities and also boundaries.

As a teacher, day care practitioner or childminder, you will encounter situations which are difficult for you and it is important that your own skills, strengths and those areas which perhaps are more uncomfortable are recognised. It is unhelpful to imagine that you will like every child or parent you meet. What is important is that feelings of dislike are acknowledged because they can then be dealt with. It is perfectly possible to remain caring, willing to listen to a child and provide support, even if fundamentally you may not feel particularly warm towards that child for whatever reason – and there *will be* a reason. For you, as well as a child, no behaviour arises from nowhere. Conversely, it is important that you do not allow any special feelings you might have about a child to cloud your decision making or become obvious to others. Children are very sensitive to any ideas they may have that they are disliked, especially boys, and also whether a child is a practitioner's favourite. This means it is crucial that you are aware of your emotional attitude towards the group of children in your care. All this leads to the main point: that it is your responsibility to be caring towards all the children you encounter. This is not easy, but links to what I said earlier, that this aspect of working with children is often not as fully discussed and it needs to be. Working with children is incredibly rewarding, but also can be exhausting and frustrating. Dealing with parents can also test your patience to the limit. It is easy to talk about partnership with parents, for example, but you also have to deal with the realities of being a human being with your own likes and dislikes. This is where professionalism comes in; your own particular prejudices have to be left at your front door when you leave home, and you accept the fact that you have to deal with all the adults you encounter with patience and courtesy.

What would be very helpful, although I am fully aware that time and workloads are a huge factor, would be the opportunities for practitioners to be able to talk through their highs and lows in a non-judgemental environment.

As individuals we have our own way of doing things, of how we approach others, how we organise and set about our work and how we actually feel about our work. It is vital to be honest and not try to copy someone else's way of doing things if that particular way feels totally alien to you. You need to find your own voice in what you do so you can grow in confidence, and in that way also find that you can accept the variations in the behaviour of the children in your care too. The more content you feel with how you are as a person, the more emotionally giving you can be too. If we think about a child who cannot be caring if they have never received care, then neither can you.

To be a nurturing practitioner means you notice the children. You observe them and note what they do well or what they find difficult; you give them some time at some point in the day; and you show that you care even by how you set out your environment. You are aware of their development and you are also aware of your own thought processes and feelings about them. None of this is easy, although easier sometimes for some than others. Being with children is an art, not something that can be learned easily but that needs work and awareness. The rewards of knowing that you are supporting and helping children during the most formative times of their life surely makes such work well worth the effort.

Challenges and dilemmas

- Remember that challenging behaviour is never random. It arises from a set of feelings and is always 'reasonable' from the child's point of view.
- Spend time trying to understand an unhappy child. Jollying them along denies the child the ability to feel cared for and respected.

CHAPTER 4

Self-awareness and the growth of empathy

In the last chapter we thought about how babies and young children can begin to feel a sense of inner security and safety. In this chapter we are going to extend this idea and think about how they learn that we are an 'I'. This is a topic that was briefly touched on earlier and there are strong links between these two chapters. How do we begin to have a sense of self and, equally importantly, how do we learn that the 'I' is continuous. No matter what our age, no matter how often we may dye our hair (or lose it), get fat or thin, grow, change our way of thinking, we essentially have a fundamental understanding that we are the same person in the same body; that there is an inner 'me' and an outer 'me'.

The inner and outer me

By an 'inner me', I mean that sense we have of being someone who has thoughts, feelings, attitudes and agency – that is, we are able to act on our environment through the choices we make. If we look back at photographs of ourselves as babies, children and teenagers, we may acknowledge that we behaved and thought differently, but we don't think that our earlier self was someone else, except perhaps in the changes we have made in our attitudes. For example, you may have heard people say, or have even said yourself, that you are not the person you once were. You don't mean that you have literally become someone else, you likely mean that you have changed the way you think and behave and so seem different.

The 'outer me' is partly made up of our appearance and the image we may wish to present to others. The latter also links in with the kind of behaviour we generally display towards others. As you will realise, sometimes how we behave may not actually reflect the inner self as we may be in conflict about our feelings regarding someone or we may be feeling cross and irritable but try not to show it. We also can adjust that 'outer me' according to context, perhaps feeling confident to display our true feelings when with loved companions. I wonder how many of you remain polite, calm and in control for most of the day and then find, as soon as you get home, that you shout at your family and generally let off steam. It is, of course, our capacity to be able to assess situations and modify our behaviour which is dependent on brain maturation and also our experiences of how to manage our emotions. Children, generally, are obviously less able to modify their behaviour on their own, and once again it is up to adults to help them learn this skill.

In addition, we know that our body is our own and that no matter how it may change (in size, shape or other ways) we know it is still ours and all our limbs belong to us. This is not as silly as it might sound, as there is evidence from studies of people with particular forms of brain damage (although rare) who can even deny that a body part is theirs or become unaware of one side of their body. The answer to the question of knowing your own body may lie in the brain's and body's ability to both adapt to experience and stay within certain temperature, chemical and physical boundaries – for example, our hands change in size from infancy to adulthood but the pattern set down to reach and grasp will stay the same.

How we walk is another pattern set down very early in childhood. Not only how we learn to walk, using our particular muscle strength and how we deal with the types of surfaces we might encounter, but also our style of walking is often linked to the style walking of our parents; boys, for example, tend to walk like their fathers. Our walk is also, apparently, one of the most difficult, if not impossible things to alter, as we may have gathered from thrillers where the criminal is recognised by their walk even though they have had extensive plastic surgery to change their features.

Being an individual

The idea of being an individual is also profoundly linked with our understanding of the world in which we live. As we play and discover, as discussed in Chapter 2, we learn that certain items are hard or soft, that things feel heavy or light, that there is shape and substance in everything we see, touch, hear and feel. We make sense of the world through our play and, as we have found, we also learn our responses to it and this, together with the emotional world we experience, gradually builds up the picture we have of being an individual person. We slowly discover what pleases us and what can make us sad, angry or frightened, what excites our curiosity or makes us turn away.

As we know, all these processes take time and one of the phases of wondrous discovery is when a child begins to learn that not only can they say 'no' (very difficult for adults) but also that they are capable. This means we get the child who says *'me do it, myself'* and who wants to try to do many day-to-day activities, often beyond their capabilities. This leads to frustration and possibly tantrums, and it is at this sort of time that adults have to be at their most sensitive in their help. It is daunting for parents to realise that these attempts at individual action and choice are an important part of developmental growth. Equally important are the boundaries that parents make on these forays into independence. Very young children need sensitive adults who appreciate the needs of the child, but also realise that the child needs to be kept safe physically and emotionally. Not being frightened or feeling helpless in the face of a raging toddler is one of the hard tasks of parenthood. A child needs to learn that their frustration can be tolerated and so be helped to calm down and gradually learn to manage their emotions when they are desperate to do or have something. A child cannot do this on their own.

As we can see, the picture we have of ourselves as an individual builds up slowly, bit by bit through all the everyday experiences we have, but it is perhaps telling that the central parts of this developmental jigsaw are the emotional and sensory experiences which occur first, and our understanding of our selves, with a body that is our own, which comes later. It is as if we develop from the inside out and, interestingly, physically we do that too as we learn to control our head and trunk before we can fully control our limbs and then our fingers and toes. So we know what it feels like to be stroked, rocked, lifted, sat and laid down, washed, dressed and fed before we appreciate what bits of us are being attended to.

The way humans develop is so wonderful because we unfold in such a logical way. Thus we need to set the groundwork for what our emotional world is like before we start to explore our surroundings more widely. Our first play materials are our mothers, and what we learn to feel fundamentally starts with them, with the rest of the family joining in. The way we are cared for and nurtured provides the bedrock for our bodily sensations and then, as we gradually become more physically capable, we also begin to explore our environment more widely through hearing, touch, taste and smell, as well as visually. As described earlier, this greater capability leads to different parental challenges in how they respond to the growing child. When the child reaches the latter part of the first year they also notice changes in feelings in the body so that toileting may commence and, again, how this is handled by the parents can influence the way in which bodily waste is perceived and the action of going to the toilet is undertaken, even into adulthood.

Increasing physical capabilities and growing bodily awareness, instinctively encouraged by many parents through playful games, all combine to support the child's increasing sense of being an individual. Even the naming of a child has such deep significance as they soon learn to respond to the sound of their name; the name is also linked with the increasing sense of 'me'. I heard a terrible story recently of a child who was hardly ever referred to by name. We can only try to imagine what a desperate sense of emotional aloneness this could cause in the heart of a child. Just as I keep repeating that we cannot give what we have not received, nor can a child feel a sense of self if that child is never seen as a self, so the child has to experience being experienced. This may help to explain why emotional neglect is so devastating to the mental well-being of a human being. It is also useful to note that physical neglect will not occur without emotional neglect. I need to make clear here that by physical neglect I do not mean the child who is poorly dressed because of poverty or whose diet may not be the best for the same reason. Poverty does not equate with a lack of love, care or nurture, as any of you who have grown up in poor but loving households will attest to. Physical neglect is when the parent (for a whole variety of reasons) simply does not care if the child is clean or fed, and leaves the child to its own devices. As is probably fairly obvious, this lack of physical care will influence the way in which the child is cared about emotionally.

The growth of empathy

By the time a child reaches around five years old, they have a sense of themselves and can describe themselves physically, know their gender and have likes, dislikes and understand some basic behavioural rules. It is not until they reach the teen years that they tend to describe themselves in a more abstract way. Children can also care about others from a very young age if given the role models and opportunities to do so, and so we move into the growth of empathy; that is, how we are able to understand someone else's feelings.

Let us refer back to one of the key ideas which underpin everything in this book – that children cannot give what they have not received. If they are not loved, noticed and appreciated, they are far less able to notice and appreciate others. If a child has no sense of self, then they cannot be self aware and if they are not self aware then they cannot associate their own feelings with themselves and ultimately will not be able to understand that what they feel is shared in some way with others. Nature provides us with the roots of empathy, but experience is the food such a plant requires in order to grow.

As we will see in a later chapter, we learn by observing and attending to what we feel and sense in both ourselves and in others. We learn by watching and babies are very good at this; what we must realise is that we watch not only what people do to us but also how they behave towards each other, including

Figure 4.1 *Children can also care about others from a very young age if given the role models and opportunities to do so*

their responses and attitudes. Babies and young children will notice who is greeted with a smile or a scowl, how people are welcomed into the home and how any siblings, relatives and indeed animals are treated. How the adults behave when in the car, bus or train, in the shops, in the homes of other people. Such are the experiences which help to feed the growing understanding of feelings towards and about others. As Lewis *et al.* state, *'when confronted with repetitive experiences, the brain unconsciously extracts the rules that underlie them'.*[1] In other words, children learn the rules of how to greet, meet and be with other people from what they observe and what they experience.

All these experiences are framed in the context of how the individual child is treated, which matches or conflicts with the outer behaviour of the adults concerned. I am sure we are aware of people who appear friendly and approachable towards others but are known to be tyrants in the home. Children, however, soon learn the types of behaviour which help them survive in their own environment. Children who are loved and cared about will perhaps more easily learn to trust others and care about them, while the child who is neglected, for example, may develop an entirely different behaviour. For example, they may strive for attention and, again, this can lead to a variety of strategies which are influenced by the basic temperament and gender of the child. A child who is indulged may also attempt to gain the same attention from other adults and children using the same types of strategies; not always successful by any means! In the latter two examples, it can seem that the focus for the child will essentially be on themselves and therefore there is little emotional room for the needs of others, so such children may find it difficult to think about them. You may also be aware of adults who have similar characteristics, who want to be the centre of attention or who are anxious to please others or who appear not to care about anyone else's feelings. Dig deeply enough and I imagine you will find a person whose feelings of self-worth are very low. As Lewis *et al.* describe, we learn the patterns of our relationships very early on and we tend to repeat them because of this.

Have you noticed how some people seem to lurch from one unhappy relationship to another, often seemingly with the same type of person? This is because we tend to favour what is familiar to us, even when that familiar thing is negative or destructive, because it is what we know in a very fundamental way and people can find it very hard to break out from these negative relationships. We can unconsciously seek out those people who somehow have familiar characteristics. Children can make friends with those their parents might not choose. A bully, who in reality is often a terrified child, will seek out those whom he or she knows will be a victim and will attract those who will feel safe in the shadow of their power.

The roots of empathy begin in infancy but the capacity to empathise continues to grow throughout life. This is because, as we learn more about our own motivations and attitudes, so we can then realise more and more that how someone else reacts and behaves is built on their experiences. We can become less judgemental and more compassionate. With children, adults need to use their own skills in empathy to understand the child who is groping towards understanding the world in which they find themselves. A child has their own road to travel but adults need to walk with the child to help them overcome the obstacles they will encounter in the emotional as well as the physical and cognitive world. It is only through interaction and relationships that we learn, for better or worse, what it is to be 'me' and what it means to be with others.

Although humans appear to have a more complex range of emotions, nevertheless I suggest that even the cruellest behaviour has its roots in one or more fundamental emotions such as fear, rage or sadness. What perhaps does differentiate us from our mammal cousins and other creatures is our ability to reach out beyond the immediate confines of our environment through our speech, writing, art and thought. We do have the capacity to recognise our self as a self and to think beyond ourselves, to reflect on who we are and the possible purpose of our existence. It is these questions that can take our minds into abstract places without time or physical constraints. In the early years, in tandem with a growing realisation of self as person, there develops the 'theory of mind' which we encountered briefly in the last chapter and which has been described by Perner and Lang as a *'conceptual system . . . with which we can impute mental states to others and ourselves, that is what we know, think, want feel, etc'.*[2] As well as reaching into our own minds, we reach into the minds of others and we begin to do this in our pre-school years.

Challenges and dilemmas

- Practitioners need to acknowledge that children in their care may need to attempt the 'seemingly impossible' in their struggle to discover who they are and to assert some independence.
- They should find ways of nurturing the children for whom they are key worker so that those in their care may:

  - develop the understanding that they are loved
  - form the emotional tools to understand and appreciate others – in other words, empathy.

CHAPTER 5

Observing and reflecting on children's emotional well-being

Because this book is focused on the emotional needs of children, I want to explore the emotional aspects of the child's behaviour that might be encountered during observation sessions. This will also help the practitioner appreciate more deeply just how much these emotional aspects impact on the child's capacity to learn.

This chapter builds on the EYFS requirement to *'Look, Listen and Note'* children's achievements. However, as well as assessing what children have learned, the requirements suggest that children's attitudes and learning skills should be noted and encouraged. As we have seen from the previous chapters, a child's attitude and their responses to their experiences are highly influenced by their emotional world. Therefore this chapter will consider the emotional focus for reflection when observing a child in any activity.

Crucially, as we have already discovered, a child's interactions with their adult carers provide the bedrock for emotional well-being. Therefore, observing and thinking about a child's learning is a two-way process which involves the practitioner being able to reflect on their own involvement, attitudes and behaviour. This will help to emphasise the importance of the dynamic interplay between adult and child. I will mainly consider observing a single child, but will bring in aspects of group observation when thinking about how children relate to one another.

The chapter will be structured around the following three headings: observing; reflection; and assessment and potential action. I will also emphasise the importance of play as a medium for observing the child's actual maturational levels.

Observing

What does observing actually mean? The EYFS talks about *'looking'* and indeed that is basically what observation is. However, observing is looking with a purpose and, as such, is a highly active process rather than the passive one the word observation might imply. Observing involves great skill because when we look at or observe a child, we are actively paying attention. We are noticing what is actually happening and this means we are focused on a child as an individual. Observing in this way also means trying to look with an open mind. It is often too easy to have made up your mind about what you are going to observe in advance, because of what you may already know about the child and, more importantly, what feelings you hold about that particular child. The EYFS also talks about the necessity to listen, and indeed this is also part of your focused attention on a child, although in practice this can sometimes be difficult because of the impact of the setting's layout and noise levels. However, you can observe a child's language skills when you are with them during an activity or at snack or meal times, or simply notice what is happening in free play. Incidentally, free play is a wonderful source to properly observe language skills as well as providing the means of finding out what the child can actually do and how they think and feel.

There are some practical issues to consider when observations are undertaken. Perhaps one of the most important is to be very clear about the reason why an observation is taking place. The basic answer may very well be that without observation it is virtually impossible to understand a child or group of children. Even at the most simple level, observations must take place to gauge a child's development and to note how they are progressing and what new skill may have been attained. On a deeper level, observations can provide real insight into a child's behaviour and their particular needs, and can identify areas in which children require help and support. Unfortunately, observations can be seen as somewhat of a chore in some contexts, rather than a requirement for good practice. Observations do not have to be lengthy; sometimes simply a note on a 'post it' when something has been noticed. Such comments can then be collated at the end of the day to allow for assessment and reflection. However, in practice, observations are often carried out because some aspect of the child has been highlighted as presenting a particular difficulty either for the child or the practitioners. It may be useful to consider that observations of children who are coping in their setting are also of value. A child who seems to be in the middle of attainment and whose behaviour causes no problems can often be overlooked, and yet such children are just as much in need of the practitioner's attention as a more obviously needy child. The child who is excelling will also need to be observed to ensure they are not only sufficiently challenged, so that they do not become bored or discouraged, but also that they are not overly challenged so that they become disenchanted with the subjects they appear to love.

Reflection

So, what kind of things might you be looking for and reflecting upon when observing a child in free play or involved in a more structured activity? A first point can be the general emotional tone of the child's behaviour. This may sound a very abstract notion, but during an observation, whether of a single child or a group of children, it is possible to identify the general mood of the child by carefully observing how they do something, as well as what they do.

Figure 5.1 *Something does not have to be obviously fun to be enjoyed; sometimes exploring and finding out can be very serious*

I said observation was a skill! There is an old song which says, 'It's not what you do, it's the way that you do it' and this applies very much in this situation. One word of caution to be aware of: the assumption that a child who is smiling is necessarily content. Anxious and/or fearful children can smile a great deal simply to cover their anxiety and to appear non-threatening to others. If we think back to the preceding chapters, we can see how it can be one of those behavioural strategies that children learn to use to keep themselves safe. However, shared laughter or mutual smiling are stronger indicators that the child is genuinely enjoying what they are doing, as is whether the child is singing, talking or humming to themselves. A child's total absorption in what they are doing also indicates a deep level of involvement and enjoyment. Something does not have to be obviously fun to be enjoyed; sometimes exploring and finding out can be very serious.

Here are some of the factors that you can bring to your assessment:

- Does the child appear comfortable and at ease, or is there anxiety or hesitation?
- Is the child easily frustrated, demanding or easily upset by others?

Some of this may be part of the child's basic temperament, and by this I mean that a child may be generally rather anxious or withdrawn or be very forward and appear confident and approachable. If you remember from the preceding chapter about how we learn to have a sense of self, our general mood will be part of that self-portrait. For example, a very straightforward way of thinking about this is to ask yourself, are you someone who sees a glass as half full or half empty? In other words, are you generally positive about things, or do you have a somewhat negative view of the world and the people in it? Do you expect to be treated well or badly? Do you tend to be very careful about whom you trust or do you tend to like most of the people you meet? No one is happy and content all the time or even miserable all the time (hopefully), but each of us has a tendency in either direction and our experiences together with our basic personality will influence just how far up or down the spectrum of contentment or dissatisfaction we will go.

A child is very early on in their journey towards how they view the world, but as you already know, experiences will already be shaping their character and personality. So when you observe, you will already have some kind of baseline on which you will then view your understanding of how the child actually is at the particular time of the observation. In fact, this baseline is very helpful as observing anxiety in a child who may normally be curious and adventurous will send a signal to you that something may be troubling that child, and you need to find out what that is. Whether the problem is simply the novelty of a particular activity to more troubling factors such as problems in the family or, perhaps, bullying.

So, back to what we may observe and the song, which states not what the child is doing but how they are doing it. Another aspect within the observation which will help consider how the child is feeling and what their attitude towards their play or other activity will be is how easily they may or may not be distracted and whether they are persistent in what they are doing, or if they tend to give up easily or become disappointed and angry when things don't go their way. Some children are perfectionists and it is very important for them to get things just right. They can become angry and frustrated at themselves, sometimes even rubbishing their own work. They may, for example, tear up a painting or scribble over it in frustration. Such a child will need a different strategy from the adults than the child who cannot believe in praise and, again, may be dismissive of their work because they think that they are rubbish, not that their work has not reached their own exacting standards; a very important difference. Another aspect, which has been touched on earlier, is the child's level of absorption and involvement in what they are doing. Incidentally, it is important for practitioners to recognise that if a child is involved in a particular activity which involves the creation of something, or is in the middle of some absorbing imaginative play, they need to feel that they will be allowed to finish the activity in a positive way. It is such poor practice for children to be told they must simply put materials away without consideration as to what stage in the activity the child has reached. To reassure a child that they can come back and finish the activity at some stage can be very helpful rather than their wonderful creation being dismantled as it is time for lunch.

To return to involvement, excellent research resulting in a five-point scale for assessing well-being and involvement was carried out by Professor Ferre Leavers.[1] He uses the term *'well-being'* to indicate the child's emotional state and for both well-being and involvement there is a five-point scale, with 1 being very low and 5 high. Criteria for a high level of involvement include the presence of creativity, attention and persistence. Criteria for very low levels of involvement include a child who simply stares into space, is very easily distracted or appears to flit from one thing to another. I am sure many practitioners have encountered children in this category. The key factor for them is how persistent these high and low levels of both well-being and involvement are over time, which again demonstrates the importance of observation. A child who has low levels of well-being and/or involvement will not be able to learn and may instead become withdrawn or disruptive or both, unwilling to approach adults for help.

In my own research, I examined the social interactions of a mental-age-matched group of children with autism and children with general learning disabilities. Criteria for positive social interactions, which potentially indicate higher levels of well-being, include aspects such as: eye gaze, being relaxed and appropriate, instigating contact and approaching others with little obvious hesitation. A low level of social interaction could include not responding to or instigating contact with any adults or other children. Again, it is important to distinguish between the child who sometimes likes to be on their own and the child who appears to shrink from, or actually avoid, contact with others, but this must be in most contexts.

The child's level of curiosity when new activities or materials are introduced, whether for an adult-led activity or as part of the play environment, is also a valuable focus for observation. For example, does the child appear enthusiastic and interested, and to what level? On the other hand, does the child appear totally uninterested or appear to have little or no enthusiasm? Do new experiences or changes to the environment invoke anxiety or distress or a willingness to explore, even if with some hesitation? This latter, referring back to the song again, is part of 'what will a child do' embedded in the 'way' that they will do it.

Another factor to observe is the way in which the child generally uses space and time. This may sound rather odd, but it is possible to think about whether a child needs lots of time in order to do something, or whether they appear to do what they want quickly. Some very intelligent children need plenty of time to think about what they are doing and weigh up possible options. This is different to the child who needs time because they have difficulty making choices at a very basic level.

Noting whether a child seems protective of their space or whether they seem to need to be very close to others will also provide insight into their emotional world. Of course, their age and level of development will influence this, as will what they have been used to socially and culturally. Finally, noting how a child moves, sits and stands will provide insight not only into physical development itself, but also their mood. We really do slump when we are sad and movements can be quick and jerky when angry. Children can be very physical in their expression of how they feel and even the way they may pull up a chair can speak volumes.

I am sure it will be appreciated that the emotional well-being of a child can be observed, noted and reflected upon, which then leads onto the final part of the cycle.

Assessment and potential action

Before beginning to assess what has been observed, another aspect that must be taken into consideration is the actual context of the situation in which it took place. It is vital that this is taken into account when coming to this final part of the observation cycle. This is not only your assessment of what you have seen, but what you need to do as your next step in furthering the child's progress (and then you will need to observe again in order to reflect on the outcomes of your actions).

Context is extremely important, including conditions such as what time of day it is. Is the observation happening in the morning, before or after snack time or lunch, soon after arrival or before departure, and so on. What is the weather like? There is a great deal of anecdotal evidence about how children might behave on very windy days, for example. Whether a child is hungry or tired will play a major part in how they might behave. Another factor for consideration is the length of time that the child has been in the particular setting and how used they are to the other children and the adults. Is adult presence consistent or have there been staff changes or a new practitioner in the room or an influx of different children? Is the child speaking in their own home language or a second language? What might a practitioner know (or think they know) about a child? What label might the child have had when they came to the setting; were they already perceived as a model of behaviour or a disruptive child? Also, what gender is the child being observed and how might a practitioner feel towards boys or girls in general? Some practitioners favour one gender over another and boys in particular are extremely sensitive to whether they are liked or disliked. What rules and boundaries for behaviour are there within the setting and how are they maintained by all the staff? This, too, can influence behaviour and expectations of what might be observed.

Behaviour is a dynamic between the child and their environment; the child does not behave in an isolated way. Other factors to consider at the time of observation are: if inside, is the room hot or cold? Are materials easily accessible? Does the child or children have what they need?

If the observation is being done outside: what is the weather like? What resources are available? Are there enough or will conflict arise because there is only one of some desired piece of equipment?

It is often useful for a practitioner simply to look around before they begin to assess the particular environment the child is in, including noting noise levels and the available space.

Once all these things have been considered, the main yardstick for assessing the observation is the practitioner's depth of knowledge of child development. The starting point is what might be expected of the child and what are they actually achieving? To consider this, the emotional aspects of mood, involvement, social interaction and curiosity all help understand why a child might be achieving what may be expected or anticipated, or whether they are not. A child's willingness to be involved, to learn and to be responsive to the interventions of adults will all depend on their emotional world, so any aspect of learning must be considered in the light of what will be discovered through the observation of these crucial aspects of the child's behaviour. Without understanding who the child is, then, the practitioner is far less able to help, guide and support the child.

From the assessment of all the evidence, the practitioner can move onto what he or she can do to support the child, as the observations will highlight areas which require support and encouragement. Whatever the outcome, practitioners must ensure that they do not simply carry out observations without attention being paid to the well-being of the child. Some observations can be simply lists of items to be ticked, such as 'can the child hop?' or 'can they write their name?'. There is nothing wrong with such lists, they can be very helpful in some situations such as providing a baseline of achievement, but they are not the whole picture by any means. It is only by seeing observations as part of a holistic assessment of the child that they will be the useful and vital tool toward understanding what they can do and should be doing.

Observations are not an outcome, they are part of a cycle of intervention to support a child. Observation is only a tool; the real work lies in the level of reflection and assessment after the observation has taken place. Therefore, the skills, insight and level of knowledge of the observer are paramount. Practitioners must be self-aware; aware of any prejudices they might have about a child or whether they feel somewhat indulgent towards a child's behaviour. Also, practitioners need to be very honest with themselves about what they know and don't know. Practitioners must be willing to ask questions, follow their gut feelings, be open-minded and ready to question what might already be known about the child. Finally, practitioners must always put the needs of the child first in their thinking.

Challenges and dilemmas

- Observing is looking with an open mind. It also needs a purpose and involves listening as well as watching. Its great advantage is that a good observation gives clear evidence, rather than supposition, of a child's well-being.
- Reflections need to be acted on. If they are filed away, the entire process is valueless to the child. Key reflections need to be shared with staff and incorporated into planning.

CHAPTER 6

Engaging with families

This chapter is about the needs and expectations that families have regarding the care of their children in their chosen setting and how they can support that learning at home. Parents may, for example, want their child to develop certain characteristics which are meaningful to them, but may or may not be helpful for the child. For example, a family may emphasise high academic achievement rather than sporting, artistic or musical abilities. Other parents may want success for their child to the detriment of their social and emotional needs, or wish the child to fulfil some of their own dreams of achievement. On the other hand, there may be parents who, perhaps because of adverse experiences in their own lives, are uninterested in what the child is doing. Such families may seem unsupportive of practitioners and may even seem actively to discourage the child or be dismissive of the child's achievements. In other words, practitioners are likely to come into contact with a range of family structures, cultural and religious beliefs and values leading to a whole range of interactions and levels of involvement.

Practitioners can share how a child can be helped and supported with families and so deepen their understanding of the unique nature of their child while maintaining the values that the family holds. However, at all times it is the child's best interests which must always be at the heart of practice and this can lead to a very delicate balancing act in some situations. The wide availability of the internet, including social media, discussion forums and general information, can also lead to parents and other carers questioning the ethos of any particular style of learning that is being offered to their children. As you will know, the reliability and accuracy of information on the internet can vary widely and this can create its own difficulties. In addition, practitioners will also have to remain confident with those parents who may seem particularly knowledgeable and well informed and not be frightened by them. This may apply especially to any practitioners who are newly qualified or are training while working, who might feel a certain lack of confidence when faced with a parent who is, for example, an early years teacher. Most parents, however, want the best for their child and are very appreciative of close cooperation with practitioners. It is only when a parent or other carer appears to have very determined views about the way in which their child should be taught and managed that difficulties can arise; or as I said earlier, when practitioners encounter those parents who seem to have little or no interest in their child. Working with children and their families is an art as well as a science, and one way in which practitioners can feel more comfortable and confident in working alongside families is to have a really sound knowledge of child development, including the child's needs for stability and security. I cannot emphasise enough how important it is that practitioners are well trained, self-aware and knowledgeable. After all, as has already been noted in this book, practitioners hold the hearts and minds of the children in their keeping and what they do matters greatly.

I now want to consider the aspects that practitioners may think about when working with families. The first thing to remember is that parents are the child's first teachers. When a child comes to any setting, he or she already brings with them their 'story'; how the parents are, so the child will be. This does not mean that children will not seem different to their parents, but as we know, experience shapes the brain and it is in those interactions with parents that the personality of the child is shaped, along with the strategies the child has developed over time to fit in with the particular ethos of that family. This ethos will, in turn, be a result of the interactions and history of the parent(s) and other members of the family. The style of the neighbourhood and the involvement of the family within that neighbourhood will also influence directly or indirectly the way in which the family as a unit behaves. In his seminal work Bronfenbrenner put the child at the centre of the family then moved outwards to the neighbourhood, and then to the wider social and political environment in which the child lives, noting that all of these have a degree of influence on what is happening within the family and thereby what might be influencing how the parents are with the child.[1] For example, the current recession will be affecting families in different parts of the country in different ways dependent on whether local work involves heavy industry, construction, etc. Redundancy and unemployment can strongly influence what is happening within the family as can, obviously, general money shortages.

In addition, practitioners should also be aware of factors, as well as a child's own history, such as parental illness, house moves, new babies and siblings, and have their ears and eyes open for evidence of any type of neglect or abuse. Other influencing factors include whether families have English as their first language, whether they are new to the area for whatever reason and also whether the child is fostered or adopted. Such things are important for practitioners to know about so that the child's attitudes, responses and behaviour can be set within this wider context and so perhaps be more fully understood. A note of caution here, too; practitioners must also be aware of their own expectations of a child and must also keep an open mind as to what to expect from children from different ethnic, social, cultural and religious backgrounds to their own. In Chapter 7 I will talk about gender differences; here again, practitioners must be sensitive to parental attitudes to their children and crucially be aware of their own expectations of the behaviour of either gender.

Pulling together some of the strands mentioned above, practitioners need to remember that the parents' own background and parenting history will influence their relationships with their child and their expectations of care and learning opportunities. Their own dreams and wishes, as well as disappointments and/or hardship, will also influence their attitudes and behaviour. They may be very demanding and/or needy or regard practitioners with a degree of suspicion. There are parents who may feel they are being judged, especially if they appear to have values very different from what may be regarded as mainstream views. It may take quite a while to gain the trust of some parents!

Some pointers for good practice

It is important that parents are made to feel genuinely welcome in the setting, so being greeted warmly is important. It can also be useful for staff to take a good look at the entrance to the setting, whether it be a home, nursery or school. Is there anywhere to park a buggy? Are entrances well maintained? What parking is available? And so on. For larger premises, is there a reception area? Is it clean? Well signposted? Is there somewhere to sit if needing to wait to see a member of staff? Physical environments are important and the impression they give to visiting parents can influence how they feel about the setting itself, even if they don't appear to notice what is around them. They *will* notice even if it is subconscious. However, the most crucial part is the way in which parents are treated; it is important that practitioners listen to their point of view and are patient with any demands and worries. It is often helpful to think about what might be driving any particular parental behaviour. Practitioners must take time and make time to see parents and perhaps find ways of meeting parents elsewhere if they are reluctant to come to a setting. In addition, innovative ways of fostering good relationships with parents could be helpful, such as social evenings or perhaps organising a family walk in the local park in the lighter evenings or a session in a local play area. A family picnic day could be successful. I see nothing wrong in organising a quiz night in a local pub with parents and staff in teams. Tapping into parental skills is also a positive way of encouraging relationships and many parents may have a wealth of experience in growing or making things and therefore be involved in some of the activities within the setting or in making the setting itself part of the community.

This leads me to suggest that practitioners remember that work within the setting is part of their lives and it is the same for the children in their care. You will have families, friends and hopefully a social life outside work. To foster sound relationships with parents and carers it may be useful to consider what facilities and activities are within the area and what outside contacts may be useful. Some parents may be involved in a range of activities such as a local choir, dance, language or cookery classes, all of which could engender interest and involvement. For example, a parent who sings in a choir could invite the choir to sing in the setting, which in itself could lead to a greater interest in song and different types of music. It is not unknown for a child to be motivated towards a life-long interest by a single encounter with an unfamiliar experience. Reaching out beyond the confines of the setting and finding out what parents and families may be interested in can lead to a range of new and potentially inspiring experiences for the children as well as families feeling that they too have something positive to contribute.

Of course, all of this takes time and often not enough time is given as a reason that only the most basic of contact with parents takes place. However, it is the responsibility of practitioners to think about how they use their time and what is fundamentally important for the well-being of the children. Time for the children's families is surely fundamentally important? Communication is also important, and practitioners need to find out how best to reach families. Email is increasingly available to many (but not to all, a crucial point) and such forms of communication may be useful. Communication, of course, is on two levels, having contact with the parents about what is going on within the setting and also discussing or disseminating specific information about their child. As well as face-to-face contact, take-home diaries, photographs and journals are all helpful. I know that some settings find the adventures of a teddy bear (for example) who is taken home by a different child each weekend is often a very popular way of children becoming enthusiastic about the practicalities of recording their experiences, but also provides examples for practitioners to comment on and learn more about the family.

All early years settings, whether they are a school or a day-care setting, are dependent on the level of responsibility that each individual member of the team feels about their role. A childminder, although working alone, nevertheless also takes responsibility for the way in which he or she carries out their role, so each practitioner also needs to question their own attitudes towards involvement with families and ask themselves some pertinent questions. Examples of such questions are:

- How welcoming am I?
- Do I try to avoid certain parents?
- Do I feel more comfortable talking to mothers rather than fathers?
- Do I particularly warm to some parents?
- Are some of these parents also friends? What professional boundaries must I ensure I keep?
- How do I feel about, and what do I do about, a parent who seems uninterested or a parent who refuses to acknowledge their child may have some difficulties?
- How do I respond to the over-anxious parent? Are they really over-anxious or am I simply frustrated?

One of the common threads in this book is the idea that practitioners must be self-aware in order to undertake positive, nurturing care of the child. It can be difficult and painful to recognise how you, as an individual, may be judgemental about some situations, but also it is very important that strengths are recognised too.

A child is part of a family, whatever its structure; seeing the child as part of that family, with all the influences that have been brought to bear, will help all practitioners adjust and adapt their practice in sometimes quite subtle ways in

Figure 6.1 *A child is part of a family*

order to accommodate the needs of the individual child in front of them. Prac-titioners need to open their hearts as well as their minds to the child within the family so that the family unit is seen as the fundamental force in the child's life, and so engaging with that family is of benefit to all involved. To do this is not always easy but usually extremely rewarding when it happens.

Challenges and dilemmas

- It is sometimes challenging to recognise that the information we gather from families is as useful as, if not more useful than, the information we share with them.
- It is sometimes hard to remember the professional boundaries that need to exist between staff and parents. However, they are key to mutual trust and respect.

CHAPTER 7

Embracing differences; the different worlds of boys and girls

This chapter celebrates the unique quality of every child. However, it also discusses the reality of some distinctions between how girls and boys can appear to learn most effectively and what might be the basis of such distinctions. A setting's provision for children with particular learning needs, be they physical, emotional or cognitive, are discussed so that each child has an opportunity to succeed.

It is fairly obvious that gender differences exist, but what I find worrying is that these differences between boys and girls and men and women are sometimes reduced to some kind of superiority battle, which seems to reflect a somewhat unhealthy trend to dismiss the skills and aptitudes of men in general and only see what are regarded as feminine virtues as important. Of course, there are no such thing as feminine virtues, just as there is not really a feminine side to the brain. It is true that the basic wiring within the brains of men and women is slightly different, but this difference is largely determined by natural steroid hormone exposure during a perinatal sensitive period. This process alters hormonal and non-hormonal responses throughout the life span.[1] In addition, male babies have an additional surge of testosterone at around two months of age, which then settles to become similar to that of girls aged around six months. These brain changes so early in life may have their roots in the fact that we are evolutionary beings. Therefore, those differences between men and women which do exist could link back to our evolutionary history.

Acknowledgement of how we have developed over millennia may help to understand why women may be underrepresented in some occupations (and men in others) and perhaps explain, too, why women and men may be drawn towards different career pathways. This is a factor which rarely, if ever, enters the discussion on such gender issues because in some quarters there seems to be a tendency to view the genders as completely interchangeable so that apart from giving birth and other obvious physical differences, there are no cognitive, emotional or physiological aspects which might give rise to different needs and aspirations. In fact, as noted above, gender differences begin to emerge early in gestation.

While it is interesting to think about these things in perhaps rather an abstract way, such denial of difference leads to more subtle and troubling issues, such as a 'one size fits all' approach to education and learning. Political and social ideology can also lead to quite destructive ways of thinking about the needs of boys and girls. I remember some years ago reading an article which had been written by a woman with a very strong feminist stance. She said that even if her new granddaughter asked for a doll she would not be giving her one as this was simply sexist socialisation. In other words, the child would have to play with trucks whether she wanted to or not. Thankfully, such extreme views appear to be somewhat tempered by the realisation that gender is not just a social construction. While it is certainly true that social, cultural and some religious beliefs can dictate the roles of women, girls, and men too, leading to some genuinely appalling inequality, this does not negate thinking about the varying needs of boys and girls in terms of education and learning in this country. Let us turn back to what we need to think about when considering gender differences in the UK context in the here and now.

In the training of practitioners, there is an emphasis on ensuring equality of opportunity for children. This does not mean that every child is treated in precisely the same way, as practitioners also have to consider the unique quality of each child. To confound things still further, there is also a need to consider some generalisations in the way that boys and girls learn and to consider the genuine physiological differences that exist between them. There are overall differences in the developmental pathways of boys and girls. Girls tend to be aware of social behaviour earlier than boys and girls often seem to talk earlier, although boys do catch up. Many boys tend to be very physically active while many girls are more interested in talking and sitting activities. Many boys are more comfortable standing to do a task rather than sitting, and I am quite sure you may have noticed men in your family pacing as they talk and think or jingling items in their pockets. Also, boys often fidget and this is part of their need for movement, which can be seen as unwanted behaviour.

Many boys and men feel the cold less than girls, and boys often want to find out how things work, which leads to them often wanting to pull things apart. Male newborns are often attracted by the movement of a mobile as well as the human face. This latter helps explain why the male eye seems to be more attuned to movement, while the female eye is more attuned to colour. This perhaps explains why more males are colour blind than females. I was amused to read in a rare example of a male viewpoint in those internet missives, that

Figure 7.1 *There are overall differences in the developmental pathways of boys and girls*

'peach is a fruit, not a colour', which highlights the differences in colour aware-ness beautifully!

Male hearing tends to be slightly different to that of females and this can have great importance in a group setting. Boys will tend to respond to louder voices as their hearing is more tuned-in to such sounds. This can have great signifi-cance in something as simple as children being told to tidy up. If a boy does not respond, he may be blamed for not doing as he is told, but may simply not have heard what was being said, especially if the teacher is female, which is highly likely in the early years. Interestingly, as Leonard Sax[2] points out, boys are also more tolerant of other noises such as a tapping pencil, while girls may be more annoyed by it. However, what makes things very difficult for practitioners is that some boys are acutely sensitive to noise, which can be the result of some disorder in processing sound, so practitioners need to be very aware of both of these tendencies in boys. Girls also can vary, with some being very insensitive to noise levels. One very interesting finding that Sax does not discuss further in his 2010 paper is that boys are better at localising sound. There does seem to be some evolutionary factors at work here as, when hunting, it is very useful to know where the sound of your quarry is coming from. Another very interest-ing finding from some research in Canada by Daniel Goldreich of McMaster

University was that people with smaller fingers also seem to have a better sense of touch, which the researchers felt helped to explain why girls seem to be more skilled than boys in this area. Of course, a boy with very small fingers would also appear to have a better sense of touch than a boy with larger fingers. However, as boys tend to have bigger fingers than girls, this may also explain why young boys may have more difficulty in threading and other fine motor activities than girls, added to which boys at age four are still developing their large muscles. Perhaps even difficulties in holding a pencil may be down to touch sensitivity, as well as these other aspects of development.

In general, from a wide range of research, there seems to be a consensus that males are usually more skilful in tasks that require spatial awareness, mathematical reasoning and finding their way through a route, and are often more accurate in throwing and catching. Females tend to be more proficient in the general use of language, fluency and manual precision, which links with the research on touch, and arithmetic calculation. This latter highlights the unfortunate idea that women are not good at mathematics and many believe it of themselves. However, women and men are both good at mathematics, but there is a tendency to be good at different types of mathematical understanding, both of which are of value as women may make exceptional accountants while some men will be wonderful at very abstract reasoning, such as in astrophysics. Of course, there will be men and women who excel in each of these areas, but this does not invalidate the potential predispositions for either gender.

Psychologically there are some differences. A study I quoted in a previous book[3] noted the power of positive relationships with mothers on subsequent mental health and well-being, and it seems appropriate to mention it again here. This was the study by Sydsjo et al.[4] in a longitudinal study of a group of mothers with psycho–social problems and their children, and a control group of mother–child pairs who did not have the same risk factors. The researchers commented that:

> At 8 years of age, the index children, especially the boys, were found to display significantly more behavioural disturbances than the reference children. A significant correlation was also found in the index group, but not the reference group, between the quality of mother–infant interaction at birth and the extent of behavioural disturbance in children at 8 years of age.[5]

This is only one study, but it does two important things. First, it reminds us that boys appear to be less resilient to emotional distress than girls, even if the differences are slight. Other studies quoted by the researchers have had similar findings. Second, as the children were rated at birth, six months and again at 18 months, there was a clear picture of the type of relationship that existed between the mothers and their children. As we know already, if a child is distressed and anxious they tend to find difficulty in focusing and paying attention. This coupled with the sensitivity of boys in their earliest years to upsets in their family life should be something that practitioners take into account. Boys and men are also overrepresented in the domain of mental health issues such as schizophrenia and also in special needs such as autism. If people visit a school for very special children, they will notice that boys far outnumber girls across the spectrum of disabilities. Men, globally, also have far higher suicide rates than women, although women are generally perceived to be more likely to suffer from depression. However, it is fairly obvious that someone who commits suicide is in a very bleak emotional state. In general, it is beginning to be realised that depression in men and women manifests itself differently and this again relates back to behaviour issues in boys and girls. Boys tend to 'act out' their problems while girls tend to internalise them. This may be why girls and women may be perceived as suffering more from depression.

Behaviour never arises in a vacuum, so the more overt behavioural problems that boys may display must signal issues in the child's well-being. Equality in this area means that practitioners need to consider all types of behaviour in the context of emotional health. The quiet, withdrawn girl, the rowdy boy, the aloof boy or the one who seems to cry 'at nothing' (in the eyes of the practitioner) or the girl who seems to cling are all varying manifestations of a need for practitioner care and intervention. What is also essential for practitioners to understand is that in the early years boys tend to have a slower maturational rate than girls in readiness for more formal skills such as reading and writing, and as the trend in England seems to be for more formal learning to take place earlier and earlier, it can be seen that many boys are disadvantaged right from the beginning. This trend seems to be in spite of the stalwart efforts of many early years professionals, who try to ensure that the importance of play in learning is carried into formal schooling. However, even here there is a note of caution regarding how practitioners view the play of boys and girls. There was a tendency in the past few years to see the more rough-and-tumble play of many boys to be signs of aggression, perhaps because this type of play is sometimes termed 'play fighting'. Panksepp's lifetime work has instead indicated that rough-and-tumble play is an essential part of the play spectrum, and in Holland's book based on her own research she identified that practitioners need to look at the *themes* of the play before ascribing negative interpretations to it.[6]

An equal environment?

A brief note on provision here, as it is important to take into account the needs of all children in a particular setting. Taking into account that this chapter is about some gender differences, it may be useful for practitioners to look at their classroom, nursery, or own home if a childminder, and think about what opportunities there are for the expression of difference as well as ensuring equality of access to resources. For example, does the setting have room to move? Are there opportunities for boys who may wish to stand to do a task to be able to; and if this is the case, is such behaviour accepted by all staff or is there a policy that children must sit to do a task? Such questions may be useful starting points for discussion within a staff team. Are children allowed to be comfortable when listening to a story or, again, is there a policy that they must sit on the floor and remain perfectly still? Is this feasible? Is such a policy realistic? Are there ways in which boundaries for sound and acceptable behaviour can be endorsed but without punitive restrictions on movement? A child who fidgets, for example, could be allowed to hold something to fiddle with while listening to a story, better that perhaps than fiddling with the hair of the child in front, which is much more annoying to everyone.

Provision of play materials is also a moot point. What is important is that boys and girls have equal access to the resources and that there are hopefully sufficient quantities of favoured items available. This means that girls who wish to build and explore can climb and run with as much freedom as any of the boys, and that boys can also play 'house' if they wish and not be banned from the home corner by the girls. Thinking about how boys and girls respond to cold and heat may also encourage thinking about where resources that may be favoured by either gender could be placed and that outdoor activities are an integral part of the daily experience. Outside, some girls may prefer to be active by swinging, going round and round or skipping, while boys may prefer to run, jump and kick a ball. Girls may want to play with balls too, but may choose different types of games. The key to accommodating all of these variables is access and practitioner sensitivity to the needs of each child. What must be put to the back of practitioners' minds are not just any potential stereotypes, but also the cultivation of open-mindedness so that judgements are not made about the type of play observed. If the girls do seem to gravitate to the home corner or wish to sit and chat outside, they should not be made to be involved in activities they may actively dislike. This is different from practitioners ensuring that a child who is looking longingly at an activity but seems intimidated by the fact that they might be the only girl or boy in a group already involved in that activity, is encouraged to join in and become accepted by the existing group.

Practitioners can also obviously arrange experiences which may be outside the comfort zone of either gender and provide opportunities for each child to engage in something they might not normally choose, but it is important for practitioners to also allow some freedom of expression and choice in play activities and to allow girls and boys to do some discovery in their own way.

Many of the differences between the genders are subtle and belong to the category of tendencies or predispositions. This does not mean that they should be ignored, but instead taken as part of the whole picture when thinking about the needs of every child.

Challenges and dilemmas

- Remember that equality of opportunity is not the same as treating everyone in the same way. The difference between the genders needs to be acknowledged, while all the opportunities afforded by the setting need to be made available to all who wish to use them.
- Provide opportunities for boys to write while standing up or kneeling. They find stillness very hard. Enable girls to climb and dig, whatever they are wearing.

CHAPTER 8

Can we hear the voice of the child?

It is strange how a passing thought can lead to general reflections on the needs of children and whether we, as adults, are truly acting as their voice. I was walking with my dog in a very pleasant local park. It was bitterly cold but the sun was shining and, here and there, were glimpses of the coming spring, with its promise of new growth and perhaps some warmth. I found myself remembering such walks with my late husband and thinking how fortunate I was to be walking in these peaceful surroundings. My thoughts then turned to those children caught up in wars, such as the one in Syria (at the time of writing), or other conflicts around the globe, or those without enough food or water.

It seemed such a privilege to be able to walk freely, without fear, my little dog scuffling through leaves, while for others life is so different. Of course, there are people who would prefer the hustle and bustle of busy towns or cities, or find simply walking not nearly exciting enough; but all this apart, I thought about the importance of peace and tranquillity, of having some space and time in order simply to be, and wished that such experiences were possible for not only adults but especially for children. Such thoughts brought home again the importance of play and how children need space and freedom to explore without the pressures of modern life and the ever-present media. I thought, too, of the picture I had seen of a boy soldier in the Syrian conflict and wondered what the experiences he had been through would do to his mind and heart. However, it is not just in such dramatic circumstances that the child's inner self can be harmed; it happens in less dramatic, but no less damaging forms, such as neglect and physical harm within this country in spite of its generally stable state. My mind, still wandering, almost echoing the wandering nature of the path I was following, turned to thoughts that some people still seem to dismiss in spite of a wealth of research, and that is the result of the impact of negative early experiences. I wondered why it was that it seems so difficult to acknowledge that the neural footprint of our early years profoundly influences how we think and feel throughout our life span. There still seems to be some credence to the idea that children somehow get over their past experiences and indeed, as we grow older, we can find ways to face up to or avoid situations which we may find difficult or that provoke anxiety. However, while people may wish that early experiences would leave no impact at all, the history of those who have committed crimes is often given in mitigation of their offences. Continuing to spin this thought around, if such a personal history is provided, voices are raised implying that somehow such a history is given as an excuse. Of course, this is not the case. Instead, the history is offered in an effort to understand and to try to tease out the threads that can lead some people down a path of criminal activity. My feeling is that if we do not acknowledge and accept that what happens to us as children, and indeed how our own history of parenting influences our later life choices, then we are denying children what they need: stability, consistency and positive nurture. Children need to feel loved and accepted first before they can take on life's challenges, whatever they may be.

I firmly believe that each phase of development is a way of preparing us for the next stage. Just as in physical development, we sit before we stand, so we

Figure 8.1 *Children need to feel loved and accepted first before they can take on life's challenges*

need physical and emotional safety and security before we can connect with the wider world. Returning to the example of the boy soldiers and others suffering through conflict, I doubt very much if they have any time or inclination to notice some aspect of nature which in other times might move, interest or excite them. Maslow's hierarchy of needs notes that we need our basic needs met, those of food and warmth, and of physical safety, before we can appreciate even the love and care which may be offered to us. If we are terrified, how can we also feel safe? We all know how hard it is to smile when crying. This may also help to explain the disorganised category of attachment where the child is both drawn to (because of the biological imperative to be close to the mother, for example) and also fearful of the carer. Such sad children find it very hard to organise any kind of behavioural strategy to cope with their world.

What we have to remember is that children need us and, of course, the younger they are, the more they need adults to care for them. They need to provide them with the care and nurture they need, together with the opportunities for exploration and play. They need adults who will provide them with boundaries so that they can begin to manage their own emotions, but they also need that compassionate understanding which I have talked about earlier. This compassionate understanding acknowledges the strengths and limitations of what children can actually achieve. There are times in our lives when we humans are at our most vulnerable and it is in those developmental phases where we seem to move from one level of understanding and capability to the next. Babies move from being completely helpless to forming a growing independence. Toddlers need adults who keep them safe while allowing them to explore and who will introduce those boundaries of behaviour which are so vital. Once children are able to use language and imagination, this in turn helps them to understand others and that there is an 'I' and a 'we' but also 'another' who may not think or act in the same way. During school years, we consolidate and advance our knowledge of the world, but in puberty a whole new range of behaviours can arise where authority is challenged and a need for independence – a breaking away from the parental ties – can emerge. This turbulent time is a preparation for us becoming adults and beginning a family and/or a career. This is a time for stepping out on a path where parents are still important but the love of another and of children takes precedence. The menopause for men as well as women marks another change where the life that is left to live is less than the length of life that has been lived. This can also be a time of turbulence, both physical and emotional, for many people. In old age we can become as vulnerable as babies once more through a deterioration in mental as well as physical health. Those who are vulnerable across the life span are those with special needs; displaying such problems as limited cognitive capacity, physical disability or a lack of social awareness. These people need to have others who not only listen to their needs but also provide a voice to ensure that they maintain dignity and independence as far as possible.

In our infancy and very early years we are particularly vulnerable because of the growing and developing brain and our susceptibility to experiences as discussed in the previous chapters. We need to ensure that we do not treat children as 'mini adults' but, while ensuring that we provide them with a full range of experiences, we also help them deal with their growing minds and bodies. It is strange that as adults we remember those who made a mark on our young lives, those who opened doors to new experiences or who made us fearful, and yet we try to brush aside the impact of those strong influences. We seem to have made the material world far more important than our emotional and spiritual world and yet without all the dimensions to our existence we are poorer and we make the lives of our children poorer too. As Lewis *et al.* note, *'We are emotional beings, pain is inevitable and grief will come.'*[1] This is not just a downbeat view of life, but rather it is a recognition that, as human beings, we will know love and happiness but, inevitably, some grief and loss will also occur and we need to prepare for both of these types of events in the lives of children. We need to show love in order to teach them what love is so that they can love others in their turn, and we need to provide them with the emotional resources to cope with loss and grief as best they can. We need to be interpreters of our children's behaviour so that we can best support them, but we can only interpret their behaviour if we have a clear understanding of ourselves and an awareness of what aspects of the child's development may be causing the behaviour.

I have called this chapter 'Can we hear the voice of the child?' and I wonder if we can hear the child's voice clearly enough when we are always so busy and wanting children to adapt to our lifestyles. It may be tempting to follow what is fashionable rather than looking at a child, who has basic needs such as nurture, good parenting, family stability and consistency.

We would do well to remember that we are also influenced by our evolutionary predispositions and not be beguiled by ideologies that reject the reality of our simple humanness.

I want to finish with a quote found in a book by Arnold, which is ascribed to Mother Theresa. While the book itself is overtly religious I hope that this does not hinder people from simply thinking about these words:

> We must not think that love is extraordinary. But we do need to love without getting tired. How does a lamp burn? Through the continuous input of small drops of oil. These drops are the small things of daily life: faithfulness, small words of kindness, a thought for others, our way of being quiet, of looking, of speaking and of acting. These are the true drops of love that keep our lives and our relationships burning like a lively flame.[2]

In other words, to hear the voice of the child; to nurture, encourage and promote their well-being, we need to listen with our hearts and minds, but also to realise that it is what we do on a day-to-day basis that makes the difference. It is how we are and the role models we provide that matter. We can only ever do our best to hear a child and we may often fall short, but if we at least acknowledge how much they need us then we are almost there.

Challenges and dilemmas

- Practitioners need to recognise the central importance of young children's emotional well-being to their all-round development and to balance academic goals with those of their basic needs such as security, stability and love.
- All adults working with children need to allocate time to caring for their own emotional needs so that they can offer the child a key person who is calm, consistent and responsive.

CHAPTER 9

School readiness?

Perhaps one of the most succinct and influential papers concerning school readiness is that written by Whitebread and Bingham in 2011. In particular, the following quote provides a framework for this chapter:

> The arguments surfacing about whether, how and why a child should be 'made ready' are symptomatic of the far deeper tension growing within the early years education sector, in relation to a deep conceptual divide. There is no agreement upon definition of the term 'school readiness' or 'readiness for school' and its use because there is no agreement upon what young children should be prepared for; in essence, the disagreement about terminology and definition belies a fundamental difference in conception of the purpose of early years education.[1]

The essence of the argument seems to be the idea that we, as a society, don't seem to really agree on what we want for our children. What do we actually mean by 'preparing' a child for school so that they are 'ready'? If we ask a group of parents what they want for their children, some might emphasise their wish for the child's emotional well-being – that is, for happiness, friends and sound relationships. Others might wish that their child will be successful in whatever particular work they may choose. Others may wish for a mixture of the two. Business leaders and politicians talk about children being 'prepared' for the world of work and, of course, it is important that children are equipped to understand and make their way in the wider world once they leave school; but this does not belie the questions: What are the early years for? What is school for? What are the fundamental principles which underpin how we want our children to develop? So, what do we mean when we say that we need to 'prepare' children for school? Dixon, in his passionate and moving book about his and others' widespread concern regarding early years education notes that the first years of life are akin to the time of spring. He notes: 'The winter is long, the autumn is long, the summer is long, but the spring is so *short'*, and that this precious time *'cannot be redeemed or recaptured'.*[2] He power-fully reminds us that a child of three is a child of three, a child of four is a child of four and so on, and that we need to allow children to grow in accord-ance with the unfolding pace of development, not keep rushing ahead in order to prepare for the next step.

Interestingly, however, I do believe that nature, or development, itself does prepare us in its own way for the next unfolding of skills and abilities. In earlier chapters I have mentioned how we learn to hold our heads up before we hold our trunks and we need to be steady in our upper bodies before we are able to stand. In other words, we are prepared for what is to come, but in a steady, logical and timely way. Even the tantrums, or emotional storms, of the two-year-old are a way of learning how to manage feelings through the support and help of parents and carers, and this period ties in with the child's growing aware-ness of self and feelings of independence. This phase could be said to prepare the child for appreciating the needs of others, but it needs to be experienced in order to be achieved. Understanding about others does not just happen in isolation.

To return to the physical analogy, we do not walk before we can stand, but this is what current pressures for children to be ready for school appears to be doing. The way that a baby learns about itself and the world is by exploring, by touch, by being curious, through exploration using all the senses and often in the context of play which, while broadly accepted to be an important part of a child's capacity to learn, is still perhaps not fully embraced in some classrooms in the push to attain skills.

For me, school readiness is not about the child being ready for school, but the school being ready for the child; for teachers to understand (and I mean to really understand) early human development and to embrace the need for the child to play, explore and experience in order to learn. There is no place for children to be taught skills without their being able to understand the funda-mental nature of that skill and the process to be undertaken before it can be fully achieved. To return to Dixon, he is particularly passionate about children's creativity and how being creative is not a vague sort of artsy gift or talent given by God to the favoured few. It is an ability inherent within us all. He goes on to say *'If it is not exercised it will wither and fade'* and I know as I have encoun-tered, like Peter Dixon, very young children whose enthusiasm and curiosity has been stifled by the type of so-called creative activities within a school. Of course, there are wonderful teachers who provide the atmosphere and resources where children can explore and try out what a newfound skill such as putting a crayon to paper can achieve. However, there remains far too much of what is deemed to be products that parents may like and which turn out to be the work more of the adult than the child.

Figure 9.1 *So much of what a child does during exploration is learning*

What is so crucial, and sometimes forgotten, is that so much of what a child does during exploration is learning. Fun and play involves thinking, planning and organising, and that is learning. It may not be immediately obvious, but take, for example, the child who has been exploring the way it feels to go round and round with a crayon on a piece of paper; technically the scribbling stage. Then the child begins to make dots and breaks in those lines using and developing different feelings and different actions. How fascinating it is to think that this occurs around the time of surges in speech, with its pauses and interruptions. To stop making a line with a crayon and then restarting it is exploring endings and beginnings, stops and starts, realising there can be spaces between one thing and another. It is fascinating to realise that around 18 months to two years, children begin to recognise their individuality, their own self space. Perhaps this is too tenuous a connection, but nevertheless all this exploration builds, in my view, to a more holistic, albeit unconscious, understanding leading to becoming a separate self. Children need to experience the different phases of drawing themselves in order to understand what drawing is about so that they can then learn more deeply about representing their surroundings on paper or other media. Between the ages of four and seven children will draw anything they have seen and in so doing will learn about shades, hues, tones and lines, all imbued with the emotional context of what they are drawing. Simply trying to copy the work of a famous artist is not really being creative.

Some of a child's most creative exploration is experienced through their imaginative play, which can include all types of motor development such as jumping when being a rabbit or learning how to walk on all fours when being the household pet dog. Building a castle from Lego or turning the home corner into a den to avoid the wicked witch all involve huge amounts of thinking, cooperation and negotiation, as well as learning to deal with the rejection of one's ideas or even not being allowed to join in a game. Such richness and all in the name of play! Gray highlights the deep, evolutionary nature of play in his essay 'The value of a play filled childhood in development of the hunter gatherer individual'. Here, he notes that play which is free, unfettered and largely without too much adult intervention or supervision is an essential part of ancient human behaviour teaching the tenets described above, for cooperation and understanding of others. Hunter-gathering was the way of life of humans long before agricultural or industrial societies, and perhaps that ancient part of our DNA, and indeed perhaps echoed in those ancient, unchanging emotional parts of our brain, helps to explain why the desire and need to play is so prevalent in children and so important in promoting skills that are helpful for living in groups, as well as supporting learning.

While we are on the topic of play: the importance of rough-and-tumble play has been mentioned earlier in this book. A very interesting essay by Flanders *et al.* notes that social play in general *'is the development of emotion regulation and motor co-ordination'*. They then go on to say that:

> the design of R&T (rough and tumble) play may be uniquely suited for enhancing self-regulation: for instance the practice of self-handicapping during R&T play probably involves the use of impulse control, moderation of strength levels and planning and monitoring of social goals.[3]

Self-handicapping refers to how a stronger animal will adjust and modify their actions in order to not hurt their weaker playmate; something I have often witnessed in the play between my two dogs where one is very large and heavy, the other smaller and lighter. This self-handicapping can also be seen especially when observing boys engaged in rough and tumble, play wrestling and so on. If either animal or human changes their behaviour, the play is no longer enjoyable and therefore stops. As Flanders goes on to describe:

> In playing aggressively with you, I am learning to modulate my behaviour with respect to yours, I am allowing your motivational and emotional states to shape mine and I am adopting a shared frame of reference.

This is something I wish I could quote to all those people who think that play-fighting and the like is all about aggression and dominance.

A potentially politically incorrect but nevertheless important factor in play is the importance of fathers or, at the very least, positive male role models. Men in particular, although obviously not all men, do seem to have a great capacity for vigorous physical play with their children. This is a particularly attractive aspect of the male psyche in that they often continue to be playful throughout their life span. Research tends to indicate that fathers tend to challenge their children to confront and manage the unfamiliar in the outside world. It is said that women hold a child to their hearts while men hold a child up to the stars. In other words, there is a balance between the gift that a mother and a father give to a child; the former gives safety and security, the latter gives exploration and challenge. Children who are impulsively aggressive can be shown (along with other factors) to often not have a father in the household or a father who is not behaving as such.

I have spent some time discussing rough-and-tumble play because it is part of what young children need to do, so school should be prepared for and accommodate this need, as well as allowing time and resources for children to learn through play. Our arbitrary entrance age of five does not reflect the needs of children and the tendency to introduce more and more formal types of learning experiences to younger children simply flies against all that is known about early child development. I wonder why this is; and while fully accepting that something needs to be done about the poor attainment of far too many children in secondary school, perhaps rather than thinking that children need to be ready for school, forcing formal teaching and learning experiences at earlier and earlier stages, the opposite may be true. It may be that allowing children time to grow and develop at a pace which coincides with their individual needs in the context of overall developmental understanding may produce the very effects that are wanted; that is, interested children who want to learn.

In other words, children need time to simply be themselves, to explore according to their developmental needs and to have the support of adults who do not try to hurry them into adulthood. Unfortunately, however, it seems as if society does want children to look and behave as if they were small versions of adults. To return to Dixon's statement that 'spring is short', is it really too much to ask that we allow children to be children and that we make their venture into school something that relates to their actual needs and allows them to flourish in a benevolent environment where they are encouraged to play, learn, explore, cooperate and also learn about boundaries? Are we adults really so caught up in our own needs that we cannot see what introducing formal learning before a child is ready can do? Sadly many children, especially boys, are put off school and learning, especially reading and writing, because it is introduced too soon and without a consideration of how these academic subjects might be more appropriately introduced.

Is a child ready for school? Again, the real question is one put much earlier: is the school ready for the child?

Challenges and dilemmas

- Practitioners need the courage to recognise that there is no agreement upon what a child should be prepared for. The best preparation they can offer the child is appropriate experiences for the stage a child has currently reached.
- Recognising that the skills a child needs in school, and for life, are best learned playfully.

Notes

Introduction to the series

1 National Association for the Education of Young Children (2009) Position statement.
2 DfES (2007) *The Early Years Foundation Stage*, London: DfES.

1 Setting the scene

1 Ekman, P. (2004) *Emotions Revealed: Understanding faces and feelings*, London: Orion Books.
2 Music, G. (2011) *Nurturing Natures*, Hove: Psychology Press. Robinson, M. (2001) From *Birth to One, the Year of Opportunity*, Milton Keynes: Open University Press.
3 Pessoa, F. (2010) *The Book of Disquiet*. London: Serpent's Tail Books.
4 Damasio, A. (2010) *Self Comes to Mind*. London: Heinemann.
5 Schore, A.N. (2011) 'The science of the art of psychotherapy', Paper presented at Cambridge Emotional Wellbeing, Faculty of Education Conference, October.
6 Schore, 'The science of the art of psychotherapy'.
7 Music, G. (2011) *Nurturing Natures*, Hove: Psychology Press.
8 Robinson, M. (2011) *Infant Mental Health: Effective prevention and early intervention*. London: CPHVA/Unite.
9 Matsuzawa, J., Matsui, M., Konishi, T., Noguchi, K., Gur, R.C., Bilker, W. and Miyawaki, T. (2001) 'Age-related Volumetric Changes of Brain Gray and White Matter in Healthy Infants and Children', *Cerebral Cortex*, 11 (4), 335–342. Knickmeyer, R., Gouttard, S., Kang, C., Evans, D., Wilber, K., Smith, K., Hamer, R.M., Lin, W. and Gilmore, J.H. (2008) 'A structural MRI study of human brain development from birth to 2 years', *Journal of Neuroscience*, 19, 12176–12182.
10 For an overview of these changes, see Robinson, M. (2008) *Development Birth to Eight*. Milton Keynes: Open University Press.
11 Siegel, D.J. (2007) *The Mindful Brain*. New York: Norton.
12 Siegel, D.J. (2007) *The Mindful Brain*. New York: Norton. Siegel, D.J. (2003) 'An interpersonal neurobiology of psychotherapy: the developing mind and the resolution of trauma' in Solomon, M.F. and Siegel, D.J. (eds) *Healing Trauma: Attachment, mind, body and brain*. New York: Norton.
13 Schore, A. (1994) *Affect Regulation and the Origin of the Self*. Mahwah, NJ: Erlbaum. Schore, A. (2003) 'Early relational trauma, disorganised attachment and the development of a predisposition to violence' in Solomon, M.F. and Siegel, D.J. (eds) *Healing Trauma: Attachment, mind, body and brain*. New York: Norton. Schore, A.N. (2011) 'The science of the art of psychotherapy', Paper presented at Cambridge Emotional Wellbeing, Faculty of Education Conference, October.

14 LeDoux, J. (1998) *The Emotional Brain*. London: Weidenfield & Nicholson.

15 Gregory, R.L. (2004) *Oxford Companion to the Mind*, New York: Oxford University Press.

16 Cozolino, L. (2006) *The Neuroscience of Human Relationships*. London, Norton Publishers.

17 Goldberg, E. (2001) *The Executive Brain*. Oxford: Oxford University Press.

18 Schore, A. (1994) *Affect Regulation and the Origin of the Self*. Mahwah, NJ: Erlbaum. Schore, A. (2003) 'Early Relational trauma, disorganised attachment and the development of a predisposition to violence', in Solomon, M.F. and Siegel, D.J. (eds) *Healing Trauma: Attachment, mind, body and brain*. New York: Norton. Schore, A.N. (2011) 'The science of the art of psychotherapy', Paper presented at Cambridge Emotional Wellbeing, Faculty of Education Conference, October. Perry, B. (2006) 'Applying principles of neurodevelopment to clinical work with maltreated and traumatised children', in Boyd Webb, N., (ed.) *Working with Traumatised Youth in Child Welfare*. New York: Guildford Press. Panksepp, J. (1998) *Affective Neuroscience*. New York: Oxford University Press. Sunderland, M. (2006) *The Science of Parenting*. London: Dorling Kindersley.

19 Perry, B. (2006) 'Applying principles of neurodevelopment to clinical work with maltreated and traumatised children', in Boyd Webb, N. (ed.) *Working with Traumatised Youth in Child Welfare*. New York: Guildford Press.

20 Cozolino, L. (2006) *The Neuroscience of Human Relationships*. London: Norton Publishers.

21 Siegel, D.J. (2007) *The Mindful Brain*. New York: Norton.

22 Gerhardt, S. (2004) *Why Love Matters: How affection shapes a baby's brain*. London: Routledge.

23 Berthoz, A. (2000) *The Brain's Sense of Movement*. London: Harvard University Press. Goddard, S. (2005) *Reflexes, Learning and Behaviour*. Oregon: Fern Ridge Press, 2nd edition.

24 Knickmeyer, R., Gouttard, S., Kang, C., Evans, D., Wilber, K., Smith, K., Hamer, R.M., Lin, W. and Gilmore, J.H. (2008) 'A structural MRI study of human brain development from birth to 2 years', *Journal of Neuroscience*, 19, 12176–12182.

25 Goddard, S. (2005) *Reflexes, Learning and Behaviour*. Oregon: Fern Ridge Press, 2nd edition.

26 Johnson, M.H., (2001) 'Functional brain development in humans: nature reviews', *Neuroscience*, 2, 474–483.

27 Soussignan, R. and Schaal, B. (2005) 'Emotional processes in human new-borns: a functionalist perspective', in Nadel, J. and Muir, D. (eds) *Emotional Development*. Oxford: Oxford University Press. Cozolino, L. (2006) *The Neuroscience of Human Relationships*. London: Norton Publishers.

2 Play, imitation and exploration; development's instrument

1 This was at the monkey sanctuary in Dorset. Much of their work has been filmed and can be seen on some of the many terrestrial TV channels.

2 Goldschmied, E. and Jackson, S. (1999) *People under Three*. New York: Routledge.

3 Orr, R., (2003) *My Right to Play*. Maidenhead: Open University Press.

4 Nishida, T., Mitani, J. and Watts, D. (2004) 'Variable grooming behaviours in wild chimpanzees', *Folia Primatologica*, 75 (1), 31–36.

5 Panksepp, J. (1998) *Affective Neuroscience: the foundations of human and animal emotions*. New York: Oxford University Press.

6 Leslie, A. (1987) 'Pretence and representation: the origins of "theory of mind"', *Psychological Review* 94 (4), 412–446.

7 Panksepp, J. (ed.) (1996) *Advances in Biological Psychiatry*, Vol. 2. Greenwich, CT: JAI Press.

8 Harris, P.L. (2000) *The Work of the Imagination*. Oxford: Blackwell Publishers Ltd.

3 Learning to be secure, learning to learn and the nurturing practitioner

1 Robinson, M. (2008) *Child Development from Birth to Eight*. Maidenhead: Open University Press. Robinson, M. (2010) *Understanding Behaviour and Development in Early Childhood: A guide to theory and practice*. London: Routledge.
2 Schore, A.N. (1994) *Affect Regulation and the Origin of the Self: The neurobiology of emotional development*. Mahwah, NJ: Erlbaum.
3 Bowlby, J. (1980) *Attachment and Loss*. London: Penguin Books.
4 Bowlby, J. (1946) *Forty-four Juvenile Thieves: Their characters and home life*. London: Baillière, Tindall & Cox.
5 An innovative early intervention project based on attachment theory introduced the concepts of a 'safe base' and a 'safe haven' as key components of a secure attachment. Briefly, this project looks at the strengths and areas of difficulty between parents and child and aims to provide personalised interventions dependent on this knowledge. The authors are: Glen Cooper, Kent Hoffman, and Bert Powell from Marycliff Institute in Spokane, Washington and Robert Marvin from the University of Virginia in Charlottesville, Virginia. Details of the project and their work can be found at: www.circleofsecurity.org.
6 Presentation at Sunderland (UK) conference 2005 on the effects of trauma on attachment.

4 Self-awareness and the growth of empathy

1 Lewis, T., Amini, F. and Lannon, R. (2001) *A General Theory of Love*. New York: Vintage Books.
2 Perner, J. and Lang, B. (2000) 'Theory of mind and executive function: is there a developmental relationship?', in S. Baron-Cohen, H. Tager-Flusberg and D. Cohen (eds), *Understanding Other Minds: Perspectives from autism and developmental cognitive neuroscience*. Oxford: Oxford University Press.

5 Observing and reflecting on children's emotional well-being

1 It is possible to 'Google' Ferre Leavers. A number of articles plus free downloads and discussions of his work are available.

6 Engaging with families

1 Bronfenbrenner, U. (1979) *The Ecology of Human Development*. Cambridge, MA: Harvard University Press.

7 Embracing differences; the different worlds of boys and girls

1 McCarthy, M.M., Auger, A.P., Bale, T.L., De Vries, G.J., Dunn, G.A., Forger, N.G., Murray, E.K., Nugent, B.M., Schwarz, J.M. and Wilson, M.E. (2009) 'The epigenetics of sex differences in the brain', *Journal of Neuroscience*, 29 (41), 12815–12823.
2 Leonard Sax has written and researched extensively on gender differences and is a recommended read for practitioners. Also, McLure has written an excellent book for practitioners She discusses not only the early years but also into puberty. In particular, she identifies the huge surges in testosterone in teenage boys which are just as earth-shattering for them as the hormonal changes in girls before their period, but often not as well recognised nor taken into

account when considering behaviour: McClure, A. (2008) *Making it Better for Boys in Schools, Families and Communities*. London: Continuum International Publishing Group.

3 Robinson, M. (2008) *Child Development from Birth to Eight*. Maidenhead: Open University Press.

4 Robinson, M. (2008) *Child Development from Birth to Eight*. Maidenhead: Open University Press.

5 Sydsjo, G., Wadsby, M. and Goran Svedin, C. (2001) 'Psychosocial risk mothers: early mother-child interaction and behavioural disturbances in children at 8 years of age' *Journal of Reproductive and Infant Psychology*, 19 (2), 135–145, at p. 135.

6 Holland, P. (2003) *We Don't Play with Guns Here*. Maidenhead: Open University Press.

8 Can we hear the voice of the child?

1 Lewis, T., Amini, F. and Lannon, R. (2001) *A General Theory of Love*. New York: Vintage Books.

2 Arnold, J.C. (2012) *Why Children Matter*. New York: Plough Publishing House.

9 School readiness?

1 Whitebread, D. and Bingham, S. (2011) *School Readiness: a critical review of perspectives and evidence*. TACTYC Occasional Paper No. 2.

2 Dixon, P. (2005) *Let Me Be*. n.p.: Peche Luna Publications.

3 Flanders, L., Herman, K. and Paquette, D. (2013) 'Rough-and-tumble play and the cooperation–competition dilemma: evolutionary and developmental perspectives on the development of social competence', in Narvaez, D., Panksepp, J., Schore, A.N. and Gleason, T.R. (eds) *Evolution, Early Experience and Human Development: From Research to Practice and Policy*, Oxford: Oxford University Press, p. 375.

Author index

Subject index